TIME

ESSAYS, POEMS, SHORT FICTION, AND MORE

RASHID DARDEN

Old Gold Soul Washington, DC

Old Gold Soul

www.oldgoldsoul.com

Several works contained in *Time* are fictional. Any references to real people (living, dead, or undead), events, establishments, organizations, or locales are intended to give the fiction a sense of reality and authenticity. Other names, characters, and incidents are either the product of the author's imagination or are used fictitiously.

In the nonfictional works contained, most names and some small details have been changed to protect the privacy of those involved.

Cover design by Alexandra Brandt.

First Edition

ISBN: 978-0-9765986-9-5

For Davane Williams

ACKNOWLEDGMENTS

A special thank you to Chris Thompson,
Gary Byrd, Nikki Butler, Jennifer Samson, Tom Southard,
Trenile Tillman, Rachelle Gardner, Kathleen McDaniel
and all the loyal subjects of Dardenland.

CONTENTS

TIME

2018

I often tell my students that time is the only thing we really have in this world, even though the cruel irony is that we won't know how much we have until it's all gone. Though we don't know when our time is up, there is much that can be packed into a lifetime, no matter how short.

My students live fast and hard, and often die young, so it's imperative that I pack as much into my lessons as possible. It's not just about passing an exam but making sure they learn a little bit more about life than they did the day before.

I also make sure that my students understand that I am a novelist before I am their teacher. I do this to put their education in perspective—that there are those who have a passion for teaching and there are others who fuel their passion *through* teaching. I am the latter. They seem to respect it.

My classroom is decorated with things that I enjoy: pictures of David Bowie, Prince, Lenny Kravitz, Aaliyah, Steph Curry, James Harden, and photos of my friends and fraternity brothers. Before 2016, I wouldn't have thought that any classroom that I decorate would be a memorial to my heroes.

2016 changed me. I was visiting my dear friend Jordyne Blaise in Raleigh when I learned the news that David Bowie, my musical hero and father figure in my head, had died. I found out terribly—through callous social media postings on Facebook—and though I believed it, I had no immediate reaction. It wasn't until I got in the shower that the tears began to flow. The train from Raleigh to DC that day was long, sad, and lonely.

However, the death of my hero, my main man, was the jolt that I needed to get my shit together personally and creatively. I'd spent the past few years devoted to everything *but* my writing career. David Bowie's passing began a shift in my perspective that continues to this day.

Inspired by his transition, I wrote a short story called "Smith & Jones: Young Americans" which was first published in *47 – 16: Short Fiction and Poetry Inspired by David Bowie (Volume I).* I also began working on the David Bowie Syllabus, a living resource for teachers and students interested in creating projects and lesson plans about his work.

I became more prolific during this period as well, picking up projects I had long put down out of boredom or depression. For a while, I was inspired to write a memoir. Although a book-length autobiography is no longer my passion, I have included in this anthology "Saditty," an essay about my early childhood.

I revisited poetry that I'd written during the years that I wrote it prolifically, primarily 1997 through 2005. Those works are collected in the section called "Elegies for Adrian." It should be considered a companion to *The Life and Death of Savion Cortez* and is, in a sense, a proper farewell to the character Adrian Collins and the parts of him that are me.

As I have aged, I've used social media to quickly write my thoughts and feelings about any number of events. Like David Bowie and Prince, I have used aliases to convey these thoughts: Ross Shady, Chico Leakes, Jareth Blackstar, Speedy Goodpecker, and others. Several essays I've included here are extended status updates, notes, and blog entries.

I have also included diary entries that I have written and letters and emails that I have sent. Where necessary, I have changed names to protect the privacy of those involved.

There are two reminiscences of a man I loved named Shane Prentice. At the risk of being redundant, I felt it was important to include two versions of our story—one straight from my diary entries, and one written a decade later. Hindsight isn't always 20/20.

I dream vividly and absurdly, and I thought it was important to include at least one of those dreams in this anthology. Just as absurd are my shorter, *non sequitur* status updates—those are here, too.

Thanks to Dave Ring, OutWrite, Theatre Prometheus, and the community of LGBT writers in DC, I continued my creative streak by writing a short play called "Message from 'The Legba.'" It was a winner of the One Page Play Competition and is included here.

It's been half a decade since the publication of *Birth of a Dark Nation*, and my readers are thirsty for more. The direction of *Blood of a Dark Nation*, the first intended sequel, troubled me. I scrapped my original idea for the follow-up but saved an intriguing passage for inclusion in this anthology. "Negotiations: A *Dark Nation* Story" sends Justin and Dante on a mission to rescue another member of their cell.

On the cover of *Birth of a Dark Nation*, in the reflection of the model's sunglasses, is another model: Zach Yorke. It was Zach to whom I turned in order to bring the cover of *Time* to life. Because photography has played just an integral part of my personal development as writing has, I thought it only fitting to include additional photos of Zach throughout this volume.

The photos are inspired by Brian Duffy's iconic photo shoot of David Bowie, which became the image on the *Aladdin Sane* album cover. My image, brought to life by Zach as well as make-up artist Brittany Clark, is an expression of black boy joy and black man freedom. It is a statement on how I used the music of Bowie to set myself free, and in turn, tried as best I could to pay it forward through my own work.

There are certainly things that I've written in the past twenty years that won't make it into this anthology, because they aren't that good or because they don't fit what I want to say.

And what do I want to say?

I've been given a gift of time. Occasionally, I will grow sad or angry or resentful that I have wasted my time and not become the author that I wanted to be by now. Yet, I am the author that I am.

Time, as an anthology, is not a love letter to myself or even a greatest hits entry. It is evidence—proof that no matter how hard I come down on myself, I've always been writing, I've always been living, and I have not wasted the time that I've been given.

I'll be 40 in 2019. I have a strong sense that I've reached the halfway point of my life. And if that's true, I want *Time* to be the proof that even though the first and second quarters were pretty good, that they were just the foundation for the best parts.

Enjoy your time. And enjoy *Time*.

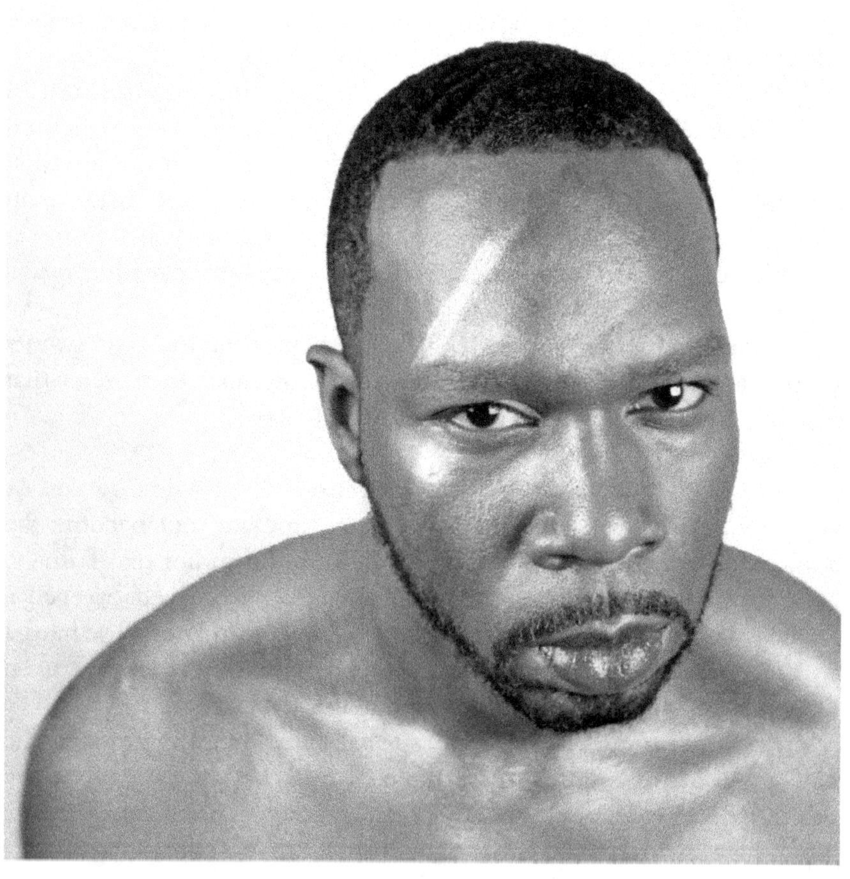

SADITTY

I am sure I was called a faggot before I was ever called nigger. I think that's the case for any black gay boys raised in a predominately African American community. Nigger as a word morphs into two beasts: one, a historical term reserved for slavery and civil rights films; and the second, a term of endearment between uncles or older boys on the school yard.

I had not yet been called anyone's "nigga" in elementary school, and I knew of no white people to be called nigger. Even now, I can't recall the first time I met a white person and knew that I was looking at an oppressor.

So, of course, the first slur I was ever called was faggot.

I went to two elementary schools: the largely (but not all) black Bunker Hill Elementary School in the Brookland neighborhood, ironically situated steps from the Howard University School of Divinity and the Delta Elite, the best black gay nightclub I'd ever been to as an adult; and the far less resourced Keene Elementary School, a quick walk from Fort Totten Metro Station and a public library. It was there that I was first called a faggot.

But it was at Bunker Hill that I first fell "in love"—whatever that looks like for a first grader.

Bunker Hill was a mostly black school that had a positive reputation in the community, which is why my mother sent me there using my great-uncle and great-aunt's address instead of our own. I remember it being incredibly diverse and reminding me of the children I saw on *Sesame Street* and *Vegetable Soup*. In hindsight, maybe it wasn't that diverse at all—any alumni I've met from Bunker Hill over the years have been black.

My great-aunt Florence Idell Houston, better known to our family as Sissy, stayed with us in our three-bedroom house on Tuckerman Street Northwest. She would drive me to school in the morning and my mother would pick me up in the evenings. I remember that first morning of school vividly. The plastic smell of the bookbags. The stench of peas in the cafeteria. Marching in straight little lines to class. This was school and I was happy to be there. Perhaps I was relieved to have something to do during the day.

I have always been fascinated with that loss of memories from before one's first day of school. I don't remember much of anything except for the boredom of walking around the house in the summer heat, and the 1984 World's Fair in New Orleans. The event coincided with a work conference for my mother, so we both attended. That's when my love affair with New Orleans began. I would visit half a dozen more times as an adult.

My Kindergarten teacher was Ms. Roberta Watson. She and my mother hit it off well, but I suspect that's because my mother was more mature and established than many of the other parents. When I later became an educator, I saw firsthand the stark difference between parents who were 35 and those who were 25 or younger.

Younger parents, so it seemed to me as a teacher, but not apparent to my five-year-old self, were so busy trying to live their lives that they missed the basics of having a Kindergartener: playing with your kid, having new experiences with your kid, watching educational programming with your kids—all of those things, my mother gave me without hesitation. I don't believe she did this out of a sense of obligation, either. I think she just thought those things were cool, and fun, and cooler and more fun than going out. (Although she did go out, and she did date, and she did go see Prince on tour and I will never forgive her for leaving me behind.)

My mom knew exactly what she wanted out of a public education for her "first and last hurrah" as she often called me. I was not to be babysat. I was not to be coddled. I was there to learn as much as possible and then move on to the next level. The foundation had been laid and the moment had been prepared for long before I was aware of it, even as I grew to doubt myself in my teenage years.

Ms. Watson separated us into "reading groups" which is what "tracking" had morphed into by the time I entered school. I was always in the highest reading groups, along with my friend LaShanya Nash (who I never actually noticed until First Grade). The reading groups always had benign names that Kindergarteners would never notice any discernable patterns in. At one time, the groups were all from nature, like Acorns, Beavers, Blue Jays, and the like.

My reading group is also the sole reason anyone ever vomited on me. This, in spite of having attended a predominately white college.

Ms. Watson called the Acorn group for circle time on the floor with our books. As she did this, a kid named Darion arrived at class, late and really dragging, as though he was still asleep. We opened our books and Darion sat at his desk. I'm seated on the edge of the carpet, beneath him, at the foot of his desk.

She called to Darion, fussing at him for resting his head on the desk, and just as I looked up and behind me to see why Darion wasn't moving, a wall of vomit gushed toward me.

It was too late. Darion barfed on me.

Ms. Watson scooped me up and ran me to the boy's bathroom. She snatched handful after handful of coarse brown paper towels and scrubbed my scalp so hard I thought I would lose my hair. I suppose she also took my shirt off as well.

I don't know what happened to Darion or who took care of him when Ms. Watson took me out of the classroom, but all I know is Sissy came to bring me a change of clothes and the school said I could go home if I wanted.

Of course I wanted to go home! This son of a bitch just earled on me!

My red plaid button up shirt got washed—several times—but it wasn't enough to make me ever wear the goddamned thing again. Not only was that shirt ruined for me but wearing plaid of any kind was out of the question for the remainder of my childhood.

My first grade teacher was Ms. Pam Harrell. My mother didn't have quite the same relationship with her as she did with Ms. Watson. Allegedly, Ms. Harrell had called me "saditty" when reviewing the names of the students she'd be taking in her class.

> **saditty.** Adjective. (US, slang, chiefly African American) Acting snobbish, arrogant, or superior; uppity; perceived to be trying to associate with a higher social class.
>
> [Retrieved from http://www.yourdictionary.com]

I know a few things about teachers now that I am one. First, we are petty as fuck, so I have no doubt in my mind that Ms. Harrell had called me saditty. It only takes one chance encounter to form an opinion about a student, whether it's a classroom observation or cafeteria duty. She had probably observed me being myself among my friends. I couldn't help what I was: a well-read, well-spoken black boy.

As my mother would say "He can't help that he's not one of those hood rats she's used to teaching over at Shadd [Elementary School in Southeast Washington]."

And she was right. That's not remotely who I was. I didn't learn any slang from older siblings or cousins—I was an only child. I couldn't even properly say "y'all" until I was about ten years old.

But I wasn't trying to behave as though I was better than anyone else. I was six, for Christ's sake. All I knew how to be was me.

Moreover, I think my mother took some offense to her only son being called saditty for the dog-whistle implications. I don't know that I've ever called a man saditty, or seen one called saditty. In fact, I think the only group of people I've ever seen called saditty is members of Alpha Kappa Alpha.

So for my mom, to have her son be called a word that was associated with feminine characteristics, well, that word was a fighting word. Ms. Harrell might as well have said "the little faggot."

Ms. Watson was the one who told my mom what Ms. Harrell had said. They were friends, and she didn't want Ms. Harrell's prejudices against me to impact my education.

I don't know how my mom worked through her issues with my teacher, but she did. By the end of the year, my mom had assisted Ms. Harrell in the creation of some sort of artsy project for her graduate thesis. I remember my mom had designed some manipulatives out of brown beans and felt. Years later, my mother would complain that she never should have helped that woman, but I never forgot how creative my mom was in that moment. I knew she was an excellent cook and baker—she had made Ms. Watson a Thanksgiving cake that was shaped like a turkey. But these multicultural educational crafts were really cool.

During my first grade year, I realized two things:

First, I was in love with LaShanya Nash.

Second, I was in love with a white boy.

So who was LaShanya? She was a cute, light brown skinned girl with thick hair in perfectly segmented plaits. She was gregarious, fun, smart, and my constant companion on the playground. I was not into sports or competition at that age (or any subsequent age) but I could always rely on LaShanya to help organize a game of "The Wizard of Oz." We'd corral a group of friends and reenact the entire movie. Some days, if we were really feeling it, we'd play "The Wiz" instead.

One time, LaShanya gave me a photo of herself as a gift. She was adorable, of course, but I refused to take it. For some reason, I felt photos were too special to waste on the likes of me. I told her to keep it. She walked away, dejected. I felt awful.

We remained friends for the rest of my time at Bunker Hill, though. We were far too young to claim each other as boyfriend/girlfriend, and of course we never kissed, but she was definitely my first crush, before I could put a proper name on that kind of relationship.

So who was the white boy? Damned if I know. I remember one breezy autumn day seeing this beautiful, brown-haired kid from across the playground for the umpteenth time and finally concluding "I am in love with a boy." I wistfully leaned into the chain-link fence as the entire world both exploded and imploded all around me. In reality, life would continue uneventfully, but I knew from that moment on that I was different. Not homosexual, not bisexual—just different. And I could never tell anyone else because surely, I was the only little boy who felt this way about someone of his own gender.

Coincidentally, that same boy ended up on an episode of *Square One TV*, the show on PBS geared toward teaching children mathematics. He was a contestant on one of those game shows within the show. I couldn't believe my eyes! Here, in living color, was my first crush on this television show.

I can't remember if he won. By that time I was on my way out of Bunker Hill, if not already gone.

My second grade year was quite interesting. I ended up having three classroom teachers.

At that point, I was placed in the Academically Talented Program. I remember my mother receiving a letter in the mail notifying me of my placement in this program. Once I figured out how to properly pronounce "Academically Talented" I actually felt special. I looked forward to the first day of school.

Instead of feeling fulfilled by this class, I felt defeated on a daily basis. Ms. Caroline Hinkley, I'm sure, was a brilliant educator. But I left her class with a complex.

First and foremost, I couldn't see. I had developed astigmatism and was growing more and more blind every day. When you're seven, what more can you say after "I can't see the board?" Perhaps I should have spoken up sooner, but by the time I did, the damage had already been done. I didn't feel smart at all. I was constantly trying to catch up.

Secondly, we were in a split class with third graders, most of whom had already had Ms. Hinkley for a year already. They knew her style, her ways, her triggers. And they knew how to bully the less seasoned second graders under her tutelage.

I had begun to gain weight at that age. There was a tall, light skinned third grader in that class with squinty eyes. He never said anything overt to me, but I caught him pointing at me and laughing.

I felt like shit every day. Worst of all was Ms. Hinkley herself. She never slowed down her instruction. She belittled you for not knowing the answers. I really hate to memorialize this woman in this manner…but…she was just a *mean* bitch. It was no surprise that her third graders were reflections of her meanness.

After a while, my mom got me out of that class. The story behind that move is my mom's to tell. Suffice it to say, I don't think Ms. Hinkley or my mom will ever be bosom buddies.

Ironically, a friend that I made in adulthood had also had Ms. Hinkley as a teacher at Bunker Hill and considers her a leading reason that he entered education. It just goes to show you that everybody ain't for everybody.

I left that class and came to Ms. Cyrus, who was really a science teacher but was stepping in to teach the second grade class on an interim basis. Ms. Cyrus was an older woman with salt-and-pepper hair. She was one of those friendly black women with the high waisted skirts—born to be a teacher and naturally commanding respect through warmth and genuine caring. I immediately took to her exponentially more than Ms. Hinkley.

As of this writing, Ms. Hinkley is still very much alive and active in several community volunteer organizations in Prince George's County, Maryland, such as Alpha Kappa Alpha and the Links, Inc.

In fact, I saw Ms. Hinkley at an AKA probate show a dozen years ago and she remembered me. At least, she said she did.

Time is a funny thing. I have no real concept of how long I was with Ms. Hinkley or Ms. Cyrus. Weeks? Months? All I know is that when they finally hired a full-time second grade teacher, we got Ms. Veneathea Perkins. You might think with a first name like Veneathea, we got a six-foot-tall black woman straight out of a Freedom School.

Nope.

We got the quintessential Teach for America, alternative certification, scared white woman.

Granted, this was literally two years before the establishment of TFA, but clearly scared and underequipped white women were available at a surplus in the late 1980s.

Did we love Ms. Perkins? Absolutely. She was fun, caring, loving, and never raised her voice above an exasperated "Guys! Guys!"

We felt so embarrassed for her when other teachers had to come in the classroom because we were so out of control. We never felt bad that we had been bad, but that we made her look bad. Heaven forbid the principal had to come in!

I got good grades from Ms. Perkins, as I had from every other teacher so far. But I am sure that was her only year at Bunker Hill. My buddy Francis said she ran off to California to get married.

Francis was seven. What the hell did he know?

One of the most traumatic incidents of my childhood occurred around this time. Thankfully, I was never sexually or physically abused as a child. I feel like every significant nonfiction book I've assigned as a teacher has shown how just about everybody has been a victim of sexual assault as a child.

Well not me. My assault happened as an adult.

My childhood trauma, however, is more mundane in comparison, though nonetheless very sad.

My friend Jerry Tyler died of an asthma attack when he was ten. I was seven.

My mom and Jerry's mom, Ashley (but we called her Lola), had known each other from high school and the neighborhood and remained friends for life. Lola and her husband had two children,

Jerry and Emmy, who was my age. I never had sleepovers anywhere else but with them. We shared everything. Lola worked at the Library of Congress and made sure we had prime seats when dignitaries like Maya Angelou visited for readings.

I always knew that Jerry had asthma. It was a fact of life for him. His asthma didn't prevent him from being a champion swimmer or engaging in any other aspects of a boy's life.

Early one morning, my mom came into my room, sat on my bed, and woke me up.

"Rashid. Jerry died."

I screamed and sobbed. So long. So hard. I clutched my mother tightly and wailed. My uncle Kenny and his girlfriend Michelle were there, too. Michelle held me as well, but it wasn't the same.

Never, never in a million years did I think somebody I knew would die. Death was for old people. My Uncle Edgar, for example. Mr. Hooper from *Sesame Street.* My grandfather, William Henry Darden. Not someone I played with. Not somebody I expected to grow up with.

If I were to pinpoint the moment when I began experiencing a life-long battle with panic disorder, this was probably it. Reality up to this point felt…real. Now? Surreal. The world felt fake to me. I felt like I was an entity trapped in a vessel, experiencing things happening to me that were supposed to be real life, but really felt like skits or scenes from a horror movie.

I became aware of my breathing. I became frightened that I would suddenly stop breathing. I became aware of my tongue in my mouth and I'd think somehow, I'd swallow it and die.

I wish I had not attended Jerry's open-casket wake. I knew that we had to, and I had been to wakes before. But the image of my friend laying in his casket, shielded from the dozens of well-wishers by a white veil, surrounded by his swimming trophies and medals, just didn't feel right. His death didn't feel right, either, but seeing him in this state, like a statue in a museum, wasn't the memory I wanted. Yet, it's the last and most enduring memory I'll have of him.

His sister Emmy was surrounded by her own friends. In that moment, she seemed like a young woman and not a little girl. I tried to catch her eye, but I don't think I did. Someone had given her a music box. She opened it and a few notes played loudly. She slammed it shut.

I remember thinking then, as I do now, how weird it is to give someone a gift when a loved one passes. Hey, sorry about your brother, here's a music box. And when do you play such a thing? Is it actually comforting or is it sad and morbid?

My views on funerals have been solidified since then. I do not want a traditional funeral. I want as few people to see my dead body as possible. If it were up to me, only the coroner and one brave next of kin would see my corpse. I want to be cremated as soon as possible and have a large portrait hanging at my memorial instead of my body.

I don't want anyone to be traumatized as I was by seeing my friend. It offered no closure. Just more and more questions that nobody could answer, chief among them "Why?"

My mother's relationship with Lola was not the same for many years after Jerry's passing, and neither was my relationship with Emmy. I always wondered if my mother felt any sort of guilt because I was alive, and Jerry was not. I never asked her, nor did I ask whether Lola was resentful.

Instead, I saw their relationship repair and grow to include international trips and fun domestic excursions. I was always invited, and I always declined.

Maybe I was the one who felt guilty for still being here.

My final year at Bunker Hill was the most chaotic. Francis and I continued on to third grade with Ms. Holmes, a mean, big-breasted woman who was black as a bulldog's nose. Joining us was our friend April, a cute gal with thick black hair down to her waist.

One good thing about Ms. Holmes was that she was good at classroom management. I never remember it being terribly loud in her class. I also felt I learned some things. Sadly, they were things debunked by James Loewen's *Lies My Teacher Told Me*, but damn if those vaguely racist songs about American Indians weren't catchy. And who could forget that paean to Christopher Columbus, who sailed from Spain with a YO, HEAVE, HO?

At the very least, I got the basics of a classic, imperial education from Ms. Holmes.

She was also the first person I ever met who showed favoritism to students because of their skin tone. If you were light, you were right. Period.

Earlier, I discussed how problematic it was that I had been labeled saditty. Well, I'd finally met a real saditty girl when I met Mallory, Ms. Holmes' favorite student. I liked Mallory, but I could tell she had seen more than a child her age should have. She was worldly, for an eight-year-old. She told little raunchy jokes, rolled her eyes at you, and had a sniveling little bitch for a best friend, Brianna. Somehow, I knew even then that Brianna would always be the wing woman in life.

My mother withdrew me from Bunker Hill before the end of the year. Things were going on at school and outside of school that were beyond my control. They were scary, uncertain times for me, and the beginning of my family's descent from a comfortable, middle class, urban experience, to a life knee-deep in the crack epidemic. We did what we had to do to survive, but we did not thrive. We slipped further and further away from the American dream over the next few years. I'd be closer to those "hood rats from Shadd" than I ever thought I would be.

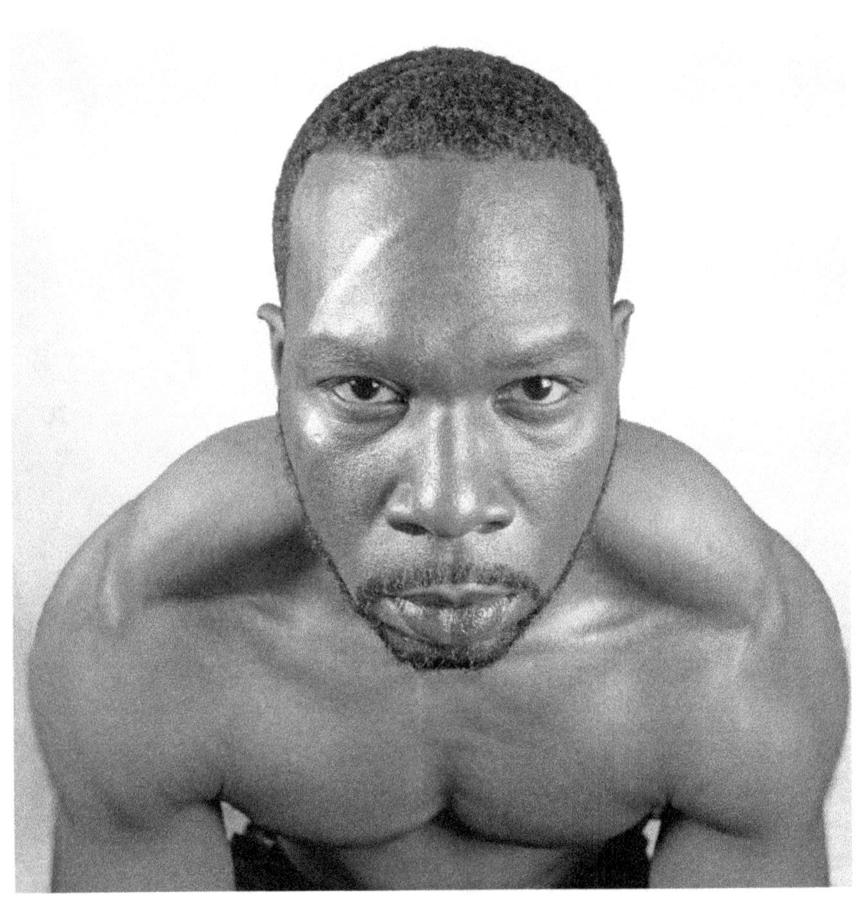

I realized this morning that nobody's ever told me
that I could have it all.
I decided that I can and I will.

--May 8, 2014

MAY 4, 2004

MAY 4, 1999

I am famous. I am respected. I am accepted by many audiences. I divide my time between DC and New York. I teach writing, somewhere.

I am a poet. I published my first book by 2001. Another is in the works. I am a bombshell. I am the bomb. My poetry only gets better and better. I experiment with many styles and somehow create my own. I am imitated. I am a role model. I am hated.

HOMOPHOBIA AT GEORGETOWN

August 3, 2013

One of my friends just posted an article about how Georgetown became a safer place for gay students. He mentioned that his first experience with homophobia was at Georgetown.

My first experience with homophobia was well before Georgetown, but my first homophobic experience *at* Georgetown was still memorable and has a lot to do with the intersection of race and orientation. For what it's worth, I believe that white people at Georgetown were far more afraid of my blackness than they were concerned about my orientation.

I was taking my second of three courses with Professor Maysam al-Faruqi, "Islamic Religious Thought & Practice." I used to sit toward the back of the very crowded room with two other African American students, a woman and a man who were a year behind me.

Toward the front of the room, a white student asked what the Qur'an has to say about homosexuality.

Behind me, the black dude says quietly "No faggots." The girl laughed.

My heart sank to my feet, and that was probably the moment in my quest for religious truth that I decided to stop delving into Islam. As you know, years later I became a Quaker. It still fits.

I don't know what happened to the girl, the bystander who laughed. But I do know what happened to the guy. I'm genuinely happy for his success, but I do wonder if he remembers that moment.

LETTER TO FAMILY

JULY 1, 2001

Dear Family,

I do not know which of you will read this letter first, or if it will even be read at all. While I have a nagging fear that this letter may be thrown away before it is even opened, I have faith that whoever finds the letter first will read it, save it, and do the right thing.

When one's entire life is spent preparing for something else, there is never enough time to do the things that one would like. I always knew that I would be going to college one day, and my first eighteen years were spent getting ready for those four years. Now, those years are over. I am in the real world and all the years of putting off contacting you all have caught up with me. I have a lot more free time than I ever had before. I am noticing empty spaces in my life that are waiting to be filled by my father and his family.

Even though I have lived a good life, these empty spaces make me profoundly sad. When I went to England to study Shakespeare last summer, I wish I could have brought back souvenirs for my brother and sister. Maybe a scarf for my aunt, a leather bookmark for my grandfather, and a mug for my grandmother. I could share the programs from the plays that I saw with my father, hoping that he could experience my time in England through my stories. But for reasons that are not clear to me, I did not have that opportunity.

I realize now that a real man would not proceed with the rest of his life unless he made an honest attempt to connect with the rest of his family. I've spent twenty-two years becoming a man to come to this point, to be able to write the letter that my family needs to see, to tell [my father's] family that I am the son of [my father], and that I would like to be acknowledged.

How can I love people that I've never met? How can I love you when I don't even know if you are good, clean-living people? That's easy, because I love God and I've never met him, either. I have faith that eventually, I will get to meet all of you and that after a while, you will be able to accept me into your lives.

Love your son, grandson, nephew, and brother, Rashid Darden.

LETTER TO MARVIN:
SEPTEMBER 30, 2001

Take me to heart.

I love you more than you know. My love for you has surpassed the petty crushes that I have ever had on those who were ambiguous upperclassmen at Georgetown, church drummer boys, or out-and-out straight men whom I found irresistible. I love the essence of you, the known and the unknown, the seen and the unseen, the man and the mask. I know this is real because the passion I have for you is unexplainable, like the powers of flight or magnetism. How I love you is as much a mystery to me as how we breathe through the air, but fish can breathe through the water.

And all of a sudden, I find this letter to be bizarre, because I am not masking my feelings behind the façade of a poem. This is all me, without iambic pentameter and rhyming couplets. This is the me that you saw in Philadelphia - all of me - from head to toe, from soul to skin.

I think that it has been about two months since we last spoke, at least that long on the phone, maybe six weeks since I last emailed you. It was a long time ago, I suppose. I guess before I go on, I must introduce you to my heart and my mind.

My heart cried tears of joy when we had that conversation this summer. It screamed in bliss because after so long, it was hearing the words that it wanted to hear from you. It finally got the recognition that yes, Marvin and Rashid are both special to each other, distance be damned.

My mind was in control when my fingers tapped out the last email I sent to you. My mind said that everything was too good to be true, that Marvin would again become distracted by something even greater than Rashid and I would not hear from him. To prove this, my mind dropped to you the possibility of coming out to our step show at Georgetown this Fall. See, somehow, the mind knew there might be an excuse, but the heart held on to that hope that Marvin could somehow save the money to come see him.

And the longer the heart waited for a response, the more the mind said "I told you so." So the heart is closed for business now.

Marvin…you do not know how deeply you hurt me by both your inactions and your actions. I know as much as anyone how busy a college student can be. But when you love someone, as a friend or as a lover, you make time to let them know that you care. I should have known better, Marvin. It's not all your fault. You can't have possibly known what was going on in my life unless I told you.

But at the same time, I expected more than one phone call from St. Louis to make sure that I was okay after my city was attacked. My office building practically overlooks the Pentagon, and when it was attacked, the skies over Georgetown were blackened with ash and smoke. Two days later, I learned that among the wreckage was the body of my fifth and sixth grade teacher, Sarah Clark, who pushed me to be the best in all that I do.

Jackie called me on the 11th. In fact, as soon as I got home, my first impulse was to call you at the only number that I had for you, whether it was accurate or not. And I did, but of course the circuits were down. Yet I thought nothing of it, because I knew your concern for me would drive you to call me later that night, or maybe even the next day.

In the subsequent days, even though I learned of many Georgetown alums who died, including a classmate, I was relieved to learn that each member of my extended circle, mostly blacks and Latinos from the classes of '99 to the present, were all alive and accounted for. We emailed and called and emailed some more until we were certain all were well. Then, we exhaled.

I still cry. I still see the smoke above Georgetown and remember the terror I felt. I imagine Ms. Clark being herded to the back of her plane as it descended into the Pentagon. I see the second plane hitting the World Trade Center over and over again. I remember my friend Jon calling me freaked the fuck out. Jon, who has seen a lot in his short twenty-one years, is my own source of strength. How can I go on if Jon can't even keep it together? I needed someone in those times more than I have ever needed someone.

My friend Angel once said that you don't know who your real friends are until after you graduate. Now, I'm not so sure. I kind of think you don't know who they are until after the World Trade Center is destroyed.

I had all but dismissed you, Marvin. I figured if you really gave a rat's ass about me, I would have heard from you, that Jackie's word would not have been enough to prove to you that I was mentally, physically, and spiritually intact.

So I was surprised to get an email from you…by the way, I do remember that I told you to remind me of our conversation if I ever started trippin'….but I can't help but trip when it seems like I am only a friend when it is convenient for you. I am sorry that you are unhappy right now, Marvin. I am sorry you don't like your classes and I am sorry you feel lost and out of place. And I am certain that there are other things going on that you probably weren't ready to talk about yet. And you know that I would do anything to help you through this time. But when I told you that I would be there when we're both old men, I never thought that my resolve would be tested so soon.

I have been through a lot in the past year, Marvin, and you were a small part of the fucked-up scene that is my entire life. I flirted with the idea of contacting my biological father, since I did a US Search and found his information. But I decided not to because if I lost any more weight due to stress, I might waste away. When you first beheld my butt naked body in all its dubious glory, I was about twenty pounds heavier than I am now. The joke around campus is that I smoke crack to stay so thin.

People use me, Marvin. I know that I have a light inside of me that makes me attractive to people. It's funny, because since I was so overweight for most of my childhood, girls never looked at me in a sexual way all through school. Since I never thought I was attractive by their standards, I have always had a hard time with compliments. I always think the other person is lying or joking. But my own self-esteem aside, again, I do realize that I'm special. I'm pretty smart and talented, I guess. And I know that my light shines bright. Every single man in my life knows this as well, but none have been able to do anything with that light but try to extinguish it. And those who think they can make my light brighter are also mistaken, because my fire is fueled by passion. If I don't have passion for the person who wants my light, it's a lost cause. After having been used for so long, I have of late decided to become married to my writing and let my light shine through it.

Your email made me feel used. You felt depressed, so you email me, since I guess I am supposed to know how to make it better. I don't know how to make it better Marvin, and in fact, I am insulted that so much has transpired in the fucking world as a whole, but you want me to stop what I'm doing, reflect on your letter, and be a good friend to you like I always am. Why isn't it my turn to be a bitch? Who do I turn to when I am depressed? I feel as though I cannot expect the same things from you that you do from me.

And maybe this is all because we don't love each other the same way. I have said so many times that I do not expect a long-distance relationship from you, just an acknowledgement of our "mutual specialness." When I finally got that, it felt cool, but now it seems like it was more of a pat on the head and a "Go-away-kid-ya-bother-me." I feel like right now in my life, I have every right to be a whore and not give a damn about anyone else's feelings but my own, because it seems like everyone else is on that tip.

I remember when you told me "I'm not just another nigga." I wish you wouldn't act like every other nigga, then, because I'm not, either. I wish you wouldn't try to take my light to illuminate your life and leave me in the dark. It's not about the quantity of my love for you, but the quality of it.

I wish I could make you feel better, but I wish I could make myself feel better first.

--Rashid

ELEGIES FOR ADRIAN

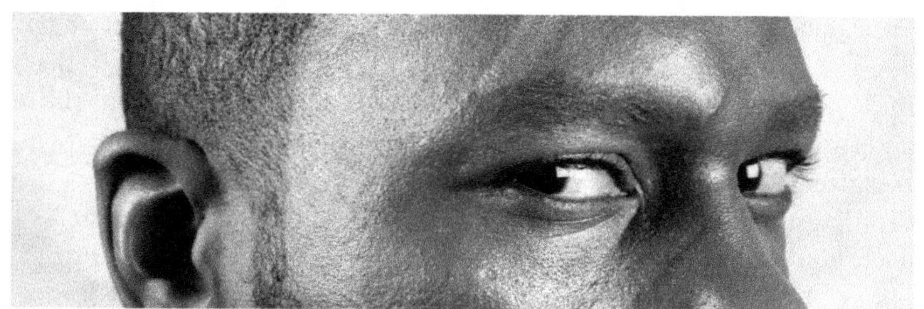

Today the hurt feels like

a tiger has gashed my body from neck to abdomen

I don't bleed, because the wound is infected now.
Pus oozes out, and it hurts to turn to the side

I can't believe I conned myself into thinking I was over you.

But it's been two months now, what's wrong with me?

I think I am officially in the grips of depression.
I have not hammered this out.

When I read in The Voice the names of famous people who suffered from depression,
I noticed not one Black person.

I wonder if the hurt ever really goes away.

i bury myself in my hoodie

because it isn't you
contemplating just
one more way to
apologize
before i go to sleep
you see, hoodies are
a good substitute for
the one you love
when the basement chills
with the coldness of alone

we're back to square zero
i'm a zero, you're just a square
i want you
you want everyone but me
and i should take off my hoodie
and put on a wife beater
but in loving you
i hide
i'm warm, i'm comfortable
but i hide
it's hot now

but i want to fight
i want to fight like sami brady
like joan of arc
like glenn close in that movie with the rabbit
like rocky
like he-man
like mike
like ike
son, you haven't seen crazy
crazy looks like writing grant proposals through spontaneous tears
crazy feels like you swallowed a cactus whole

crazy acts like unsolicited refunds just so i won't have to take a chance at putting another book in your hand
crazy feels like loving your tall ass anyway
crazy feels like loving your bald ass anyway
crazy feels like loving your ass and knowing it's not your best asset anyway
crazy is writing poems again – any damn way

fuck you for telling me not to throw around the word love

my hoodie can be pulled down over my face and hide
and hide
and sneak attack your ass
like sss sss
and the heat of the hoodie makes me sweat about the neck
and it's hot
and
and
and

i bury myself in you
and die thirty-one heat strokes
in the twenty-ninth level of hell
chillin with Lucifer
bargaining
for the chance to be reborn
as something
that belongs
just to you

if i got

rich and
could fly to
you
every week
end
would you
be
my man
then?

thanks…

candlelight and cloth napkins
my best china
wine glasses
i made/was:
stuffing
    that comforted you
ham
    that sustained you
greens
    that enriched you
yams
    that sweetened you
rolls
    that filled you
cranberry sauce
    i accepted the bitter with the sweet
but you
were the turkey

collage poem

All at once I knew -- I knew at once -- I knew he needed me

An empty room is merciless, don't be surprised if I confess:
I sometimes have the tendency to look at you
…religiously

So many nights…
So many dreams…
I shall not envy lovers, but long for what they share.

What the hell am I doing here?

My beating heart wants you
And my empty arms need you
You touch me; I hear the sound of mandolins
You are so beautiful to me
You kiss me; with your kiss my life begins
You're spring to me
You're everything I need
…all things to me
Nothing even matters to me

Who would have thought his love could be so good?

Can't you see you're everything I hoped for?
If there's a thing that you need, I'd give you the breath that I breathe
Don't you know you're life itself?
I don't care if it hurts.
Just hold me, hold me, hold me, hold me…

Nothing even matters to me
You're part of my identity
You've really got…
You've really got a…

…I don't belong here.
What the hell am I doing here?

the knot inside me grows

the more i know
i like you
but you have a man
who certainly understands why i would
because
well
look at you, man

you might not see what i do, but
trust
when i say that you are beautiful
i choose words carefully
and unveil them like new treasures

you know me…okay
so far
i want to know you better because
the knot inside my stomach grows the more i know
that i could really really love you
but you're not leaving him any time soon
and
i
am not
going
to cry
even as *poetry man* plays

and i split inside myself once
i am half
and each half is half
and each half is half
and i am decimated into a trillion tear sized pieces of myself
because i am not that kind of man

you are his
yet you run your fingers through my hair

the last time someone did that
i was a fetish
and i shaved myself so it wouldn't happen again
but you reached
and you caressed
and i allowed
and i touched
and i caressed
and i knew i was wrong

but i see you and my heart decides not to talk to my mind about this situation
because my mind has turned into a puddle of pieces of a mind
because i was a wreck last night
and cried and cried and cried
until i wasn't even myself anymore
i was a dream
a dream that you threw a pillow and a blanket at me and gave me your couch
yet i still didn't know if your man was at home
so i woke
and crept
and stared at your body while you slept
and i didn't see him
but i didn't see me either
i was in the shadows
waiting
fucking longing

and the knot inside my motherfuckin stomach grows the more i motherfuckin know
that i love you
even as *poetry man* plays
i won't let you see a single goddamn tear
even though i'd kill to have you near
around
inside
my tears create the rolling tide

Elegy for Tymex

tick tock he don't stop
tick tock he don't stop
tick
tock
he
just don't stop
Today I found out that tymex died
time did not run out for tymex
tymex did not run out of time
tymex outran time
tick
tock
he still can't be stopped
tymex
keeps on
slipping
slipping, slipping
into the future
his soul was released
escaped from the prison of
his hourglass
his sands scattered throughout
the ages
his soul now enmeshed with
time
he was there when
the first drum sticks were made
I hear his laughter in my heartbeat

Vertigo

Sucker for dreadlocks
That's what I am
Your dreads and your skin and your eyes
Your voice
Psychically whipped on our first encounter

The way you called me man
The way you looked at me
Your ways
I could feel you
Not figuratively
Not just physically
But mentally, I could feel you
That astral cord, I think I saw it

You put the money on the countertop
When you answered the phone
But you picked my change back up and put it in my hand
Contact

You know where I live
Have you seen me before?
I'm your secret fan
How close do we live to each other?
I'm your secret admirer
Never thought I'd have the guts to have a conversation with you
My, how times have changed
I've grown a lot, but you've still been there
Waiting for me, perhaps?

Your eyes
There's just something…
I had no fear looking into them
Your eyes

I couldn't see anything but them
Then I saw your face
Then I saw your dreads
Then I heard your voice
Then I felt your fingertips in my palm
And then I saw the cord
And you called me "man"
And we said good-bye

I'll be back to see you again
And this time I'll find out your name

maya's elegy

she was the beauty that existed in
the harshness of words
and the anger of arguments

she was the elegance in silence

she was…

the colors of spring

(Spring 2000)

white sky pours crystal clear rain
unrefined passion for the canary sun
rain turning gray in the virgin spring day
sky's gentle gifts touching the brown earth
turning the sun orange with rage
creating night, black and passionless

season is but a week old but the fever hits anyway

i want and he wants and you want
but what do we want
for we are we, not three
three become we as the sun breaks through
the blinds
fiery bars prevent us from leaving the dark cell
three bodies with one mind

we
lay as triplets in the womb
he
tolerates the masochistic fires
of touching her
her response more bitter than the
winds driving the rain: silence
the rain
causing
me
to reminisce on earlier lives
earlier loves
because I feel his touch through her
as if her body is merely the conductor
emotions misdirected to me
she

bound in primordial cords of iron
never letting him in
only letting him pass through
to me
i asked not to receive his blessings
but she transformed them into something more
than she could handle
overflowing devotion, confused when it reaches me
confused, because it is not for me
passions hiding themselves in my gut
festering and multiplying
yielding ideas of "thisistoogoodtobetrue"
laying at the foot of her bed
we become trapped in the elements
earthly bodies containing passion's fire
caged by the rain and lulled to sleep by the wind
icy air giving us no choice but to rely on one another
the air lays like a brick on our chests
and we listen to the soil become mud outside

autumn is spring in disguise
for death is not the opposite of life
but its continuation
the colors are the same, only muted and hidden by one another
the death of sleep never overtakes any of the three
because dreams did live on that day
and proved that not all dreams are too good to be true
dreams are a continuation of reality
harsh reality
nightmares
three is always an odd number
no matter how you slice it
odd man out
i leave

black light fandango

(March 28, 2001)

dear sir and ma'am:

under the black light everything felt right
wish it could have lasted all night
three parts and three hearts and no false starts on that night
(this is no explication but a dedication to him and her and me)
three thirsty souls in the center of a sea
of bodies

like two sharks we encircled her
obeying the Miami bass
we grinded and freaked
and grinded and freaked
like ticking, like tocking
like grandfather clocking
like sucking and fucking we wished we were doing
her and me at the same time
so when we came together (to dance)
you got a snake in your hips and started to prance

you'd never been in a circle of three degrees
a circle of amour, not knowing what was in store
it was just a fucking party and we were just freaking this girl,
this girl was the last one on earth because she gave me my first hard
on in years
and i had no fears, even if "oh, shit! what if I am straight?"

through the stench of cigarettes and sweat, i still made you and her
wet
we encircled her
you touched my arm
i touched your hand
and suddenly we three understand

if this ever could *really* happen
it could only be her, you, and me
only that night

the crowd disappears around us and all that's left is the black light
stranding three bodies in the black sea –
just her, you, and me
i touch you, you touch me, we touch she but
does she even need to be there for us to be aware
of the erectile function unifying our conjunction
we are fucking each other through her but
does she feel the prick, does she ride it, does she feel like a queen
inspiring the manhood of two to arise in between
you cannot look me in the eyes, ashamed at the blatant display of lust
that has caused this show
ashamed that
we each had someone else but they didn't know
that she was the only woman that could make me think twice
and i was the only man that could make you think twice
and twice plus twice was about to get *real* nice
raw energy bubbling under skin threatening to explode
we were live we were hype we were the essence of sex
fluid crowds evaporating to reveal
you and you and i, he and she and me, girl and guy and guy
we are free
love: me

alive

(September 13, 2001)

we were not supposed to
inherit a world like this

on Wisconsin avenue
i "worked"
and while on i.m.
i was told that two planes had just
crashed
into the world trade center towers
on purpose

yeah, sure

the conference room filled with
nonbelievers
who watched the revolution unfold
it was televised

and jon called me
(he never calls me)
bewildered that he had seen the second plane
crash into the other tower
in living color
on live television
on purpose

yeah

and i went to washington post
dot com
and the footage was already available
and i saw it
the plane and then

the orange globe of fire
there just wasn't enough time
for the shock to hit me
when we noticed the blackened horizon
the pentagon had been slashed
it was only later that i learned
sarah clark's ashes were
now part of the skies above the potomac
she had been herded to the back of the airplane
by the enemy
transforming from a chaperone
to surrogate mother for asia cottom's last moments

the towers collapsed
and we fled from wisconsin avenue
i could not stop crying
i have not stopped crying
my destiny was raped
my future was rendered uncertain
suddenly, i might have to cast away
my pen and paper
in favor of a rifle
not to protect my country
but to protect my destiny
all of a sudden that georgetown degree
doesn't mean as much
when bodies are falling from the sky
but i am alive
j.j.... malcolm... lincoln... jacques-phillipe... blythe... amanda...
desiree... damien... tawan... emily... little chris... angel... crystal...
james... oliver... jorge... kalshelia... jason...
we are alive
we escaped from the towers and the pentagon
we are like that
we are greater than survivors
we are the chosen
together...we exhale
wipe the sweat

and begin to work

a thank you note

for t.d.

i am flattered by
the mention in
your poem
even though
you hate
my guts

Forgotten Dream

Winds
Paper walls
Paper buildings
Leaves
Funny-faced heroin addict
Two-dimensional
A dream, still
Phone call to the dealer
Cashmere sweater
Swiftly moving clouds
Screeching brakes
Man/boy running, stops, speaks, runs
Still remembering
The feel of cashmere

Probate

Cacophonies of silence fill this place.
My eardrums burst with ev'ry muted shout,
Though fear shall not appear upon my face.

I represent the thousands of my race
Who know the pain of which I talk about.
Cacophonies of silence fill this place

And I daren't move; not even for a pace.
New families could quickly cast me out,
Though fear shall not appear upon my face.

Seven stand, though more began the race;
Seven strong – weary, but still stout.
Cacophonies of silence fill this place.

From bloody anchor to the bloody ace,
Our grit – do not mistake it for a pout.
Though fear shall not appear upon my face,

I march across the sands bearing the mace.
Who knows the pain of which I talk about?
Cacophonies of silence fill this place…
Though fear shall not appear upon my face.

i am wondering how my male cat knew to go downstairs and watch football while my female cat knew to stay in the living room with the women. i am wondering why in 23 years i never knew where to sit.

sissy is in her eighties now. aunt dora is the youngest; she could be an older sister of my mother. my grandmother is here, and pa-pa is still in the home. ruth and deacon robinson have come. the deacon and uncle bobby immediately retire to the basement, with one of the cats, to watch the football game. i wonder how he knew.

kenny left. he dropped off grandma and gave the good "peace out."

in the natural order of things, the men watch football in the basement and the women stay upstairs. generation x-y-z always did something together. usually, just watching television in someone's bedroom.

this year, i was alone.

sissy is in her eighties, grandma is in her seventies, and pa-pa is in the home.

kenny left.

the deacon led the prayer, and the natural order progressed – men and male cat downstairs, women and female cat upstairs, and me.

i finished my meal and went where generation x-y-z would have gone any other holiday. i watched television in a free room.

i fell asleep.

twenty years from now, i woke up, and they were all gone.

april fourth, nineteen sixty-eight

is this a jaw i see, so square and perfect,
barely containing the word "dream?"

his jaw, so perfect.
i must destroy it, even though the unhappy

task will be credited to a man with
three names, for assassins, if they

are successful, always have three
names. if they fail, they are just

john hinckley. i see his jaw, and i
must pierce it, with every ounce of

force behind me. i will not get the
credit for causing the gaping wound,

nor will they report decades later
that i went through his neck,

taking a carotid shower along the
way. they will not tell their children

that i sliced his spinal cord, so simply,
as though it were tissue paper.

and they will not remember that i
finally rested in his shoulder blade,

as though it were a womb. i fell
asleep there.

hold me/accountable

i
so
rarely

write poems anymore

because maybe

i don't feel as deeply as i once did
about love
and men
and love affairs
and possibilities
somewhere along the line i just
stopped.

i have not kissed someone i was in love with in at least three years
and don't ask me how long before then

but even he didn't get a poem

—

i fucked up

again and again

i am vitriolic and venomous and awful

i freeze you out

and for some reason

for whatever reason

for any reason

i come back and you let me and you're so foolish for doing that why would you do that?

but i love you.

i never hit you, but i hurt you.

i hurt you because my father hurt me and I am too much of an idiot to recognize the patterns until it's too late.

i am the man that my father did not raise,
and somehow i became him anyway.

throw me a lifeline.
i don't want to drown.

maybe i am still a boy.

—

make me:

use my words to explain
don't give up on me
please don't give up on me
i don't know what to do
i just know that i love you

hold me
breathe your words on the back of my neck
sign this covenant on my spine with your fingertips

hold me accountable

expect the man that i said i want to be

don't give the bastard a pass

The Cure

For eight hours a day, you see me.
The real me.
I've only ever been one person, consistently, an acquired taste, for better or for worse.
Just me, authentically.
Imagine that, in this century.

I've always performed well in the straight male market.

On and on our brotherhood must flow

On and on our brotherhood must flow,
From darkness into agape's light,
Even though you weren't supposed to know.

Fingers betray damning secrets, although
I know that what's happened isn't right;
On and on our brotherhood must flow.

Simmering, bubbling, years and decades go
Twisting into ulcerous, knotted fright
Even though you weren't supposed to know.

A paragon of Plato's earthly show
That can never ascend to Venus's height.
On and on our brotherhood must flow

When we speak, my entire life's aglow
Though playful banter never carries bite--
Even though you weren't supposed to know

You will never know all that I know.
You will never read all that I write.
On and on our brotherhood must flow,
Even though you weren't supposed to know.

i touch my face

in comfort

i try not to think about all the men i've wanted to touch me

in a cruel twist of fate
the main one i want to touch me every day
touches me every day

i touch my face
in comfort

he ain't the main one
though

he's just the one i see every day

and i don't know why this one straight nigga
be touchin me
massaging my shoulder
grabbing me by the waist
reaching in my pocket for fun

my actual pocket – that was not a metaphor

i touch my face
in comfort

why you in my space?

and i try to forget that he treats everyone the same way

in that minute, we are.

i want you to love me like james baldwin loved malcolm x
longing
an aching love like
if you could just get my attention

touch
my
face

I don’t want to be alone

let me sleep beside you: a fantasy in seven days

sunday

your daughter's scalp
is freshly greased.
it was your turn, this week,
but she likes you better.
for that, at least.

the sweet fragrance is still on your fingertips
when you come to bed.

freshly showered,
i lotion myself.

you enter our bedroom wearing
a smile most think is a sneer,
at best a smirk,
but i know better.

it's just your face.

we learned years ago to relax on sundays.
mondays will always come.
there is no need to be anxious.

so we ritualized our relaxation.
i lotion myself.
in silence, you strip to your black boxer briefs.
you lay on your stomach
in patience.

i get to you in time.

it's not massage oil—just lotion
unscented. plain.
rubbed between my palms and
rubbed onto your feet and
kneaded into your calves
and thighs
and back
and shoulders
and neck
and arms.

i love you.

taking care of you is all i ever wanted.

"thank you," you say for the 99th week.

with soft arms and semi-erections intertwined,
i sleep beside you.

monday

"put that thing away," i say.

you don't. you need it.
you don't say it, but i know it.

you are an extrovert who loves an introvert
and your smartphone is the compromise.

you never complain about our quiet time together,
because you love me,
and i never complain when you need your social time
with your boys
or with the frat
who i trust
because they're my frat, too,

and maybe they like me a little more than they like you
anyway.

but put that thing away.

i lean my head on your shoulder and whisper it to you.

you smirk. you resist.

i kiss your shoulder and my hand traces a path up your leg
to the waistband of your basketball shorts

put that thing away.

you refuse, and in a swift motion
your penis is in my hand.
you exhale sharply. my fingers flex, then tighten
around your shaft.

as i massage you, you whisper/laugh
put that thing away.

moments after your climax,
and your clean-up,
you whisper
"i love you"
and i whisper
"i know."

you sleep beside me
and i put that thing away.

tuesday

we find out
brother jones
from beta chapter died
around seven that evening

you kick yourself
because you didn't go visit him at the home
i try to convince you that
his time was his time

but you don't want to hear it
you cry a little, i cry a little
and I hold you until you fall asleep
beside me

wednesday

i've never been good with money.
you know that.
stop yelling.

i already know the seriousness.
i fucked up.

years later, i'm still getting used to
additional people and
additional responsibilities and
the cost of food
and field trips
and braces
and it's all
just
so
much
that sometimes i just want to spend a little something on myself
that i deserve nice things
sometimes.

it's got nothing to do with you.

if one can grasp it,
it's got everything to do with me being an only child.

don't you dare call me spoiled.
and you leave my mama out of this.

i'll make this right.
i'll find the money.

i love you.
i said i love you.

you grumble a response and
cover yourself with your half of the sheet,
probably a little more.

i turn the light out and
take my half.

back to back.

at some point,
i sleep beside you.

thursday

kids on kids
piling into this king-sized bed.
not mine, yours.
ours, surely.
but I was going to be child-free.

i knew at a certain age that
if i was going to live with
homophobia and
discrimination
and potential hate crimes
that the least I could do was
enjoy every bit of my own
discretionary
income.

male privilege would ensure my salary.
gay privilege would ensure i kept it.
no kids.

then came you.
kids on kids.
piling into my king-sized bed.
somehow falling asleep in the valley between us
with their feet in my face
and their elbows in my side.

i glance over at you.
you're staring at me, not smirking, but smiling.

"i love you," you whisper.

i smile.
kids on kids:
"i love you, too."

i sleep beside you.

friday

the kids are with their grandparents.

i'm by myself.

we will only be apart for a night, but you
insist
on Skyping me.
you're only two hours away.
just a late business trip.

but you insist.

we talk, and we giggle, and we talk

just like how it was when we were in our twenties

you show me yours, i show you mine

we climax together

we log out

we sleep beside each other in our minds

saturday

you come home
by surprise

i am writing, writing, writing

you are waiting, waiting, waiting

and you finally

strip

and you close my laptop

and you

kiss

me

on my neck

and i love, love, love

it

and

this

and

you

you are my fantasy in seven days

we come before Saturday Night Live

and we rest

naked

and you let me sleep beside you

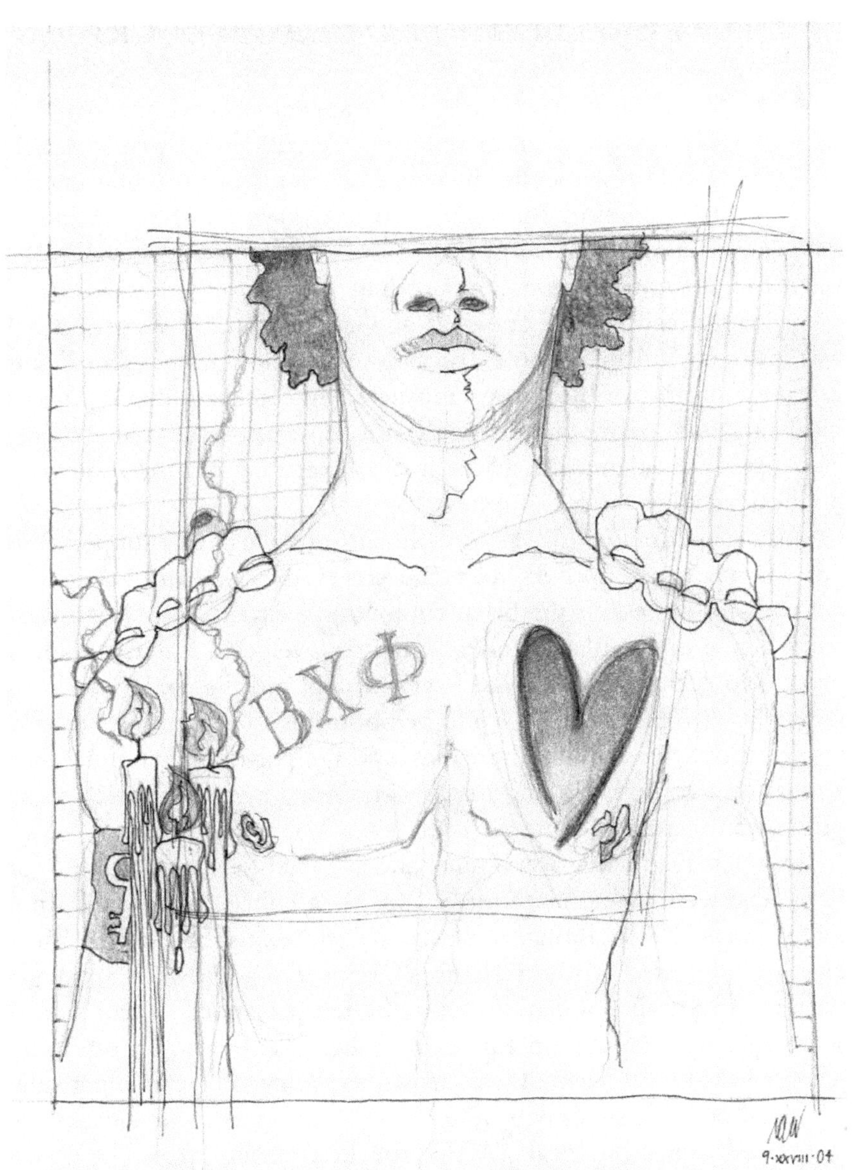

Prototype Cover for Lazarus *by Neil Wade.*

EXCERPT FROM *DISCRETION*

THE FIRST DRAFT OF *LAZARUS*, BASED ON A PLAY CALLED *BEHIND CLOSED DOORS*

The razor-sharp words of strangers echoed through my sophomore year in college. A passionate poet's words would reverberate through my being from the first night I met him until the night we parted ways. And by the end of the year, my life would be ripped apart and placed back together by the men who would become my brothers, all with only their words.

I had already spent one year at Georgetown University, and I was in love with the school. It was by no means perfect, but it was just the right mix of black consciousness and black snobbery. I was a local boy, not poor, but definitely not as well off as many of my classmates. Academically, I was not a superstar. My interests were political activism and community outreach. One thing my father taught me before he left was how much fun college was supposed to be. He went to school in Massachusetts in the 70's, and he used to tell me how close-knit the black community was there. My dad used to be active in the Black Student Union as well as a fraternity, and I used to look through his drawers and trunks and find old pictures of happy black folks with Afros and bell-bottoms. I remember his zany stories about the women, the rallies, and the parties. It sounded like a great time to be black and male, even during a time in which to be both meant certain inequity.

We left Dad when I was nine, and all I had left by the time I got to college were vague memories of his own college memories. In a lot of ways, I was looking for his college experience rather than creating my own. My bitterness about Georgetown's apathetic African American population made my temper short. I had gained somewhat of a reputation for saying exactly what was on my mind when I felt like it. While I was known for being on the militant side, I had calmed down enough by the end of the year to be elected the Vice-President of the local NAACP for the following year.

So, by the beginning of my sophomore year, I had quite a name for myself. Upperclassmen, especially those in the NAACP, respected me, and I was committed to learning all that I could from them. My first year at Georgetown was one of growth. The next year was one of work.

Delta Sigma Theta Sorority had the honor of throwing the first major event of the year, the Crimson Cipher. Every year, the Deltas threw this spoken word event to highlight the talented poets at Georgetown. There were not a lot of black people at Georgetown, but we usually supported the big events in larger numbers than one would think. Five minutes after eight o'clock, a safe time to arrive at an evening event and still get a seat, I noticed a small crowd had already gathered. It appeared that the freshman, who had not yet broken out of the habit of traveling in packs, had already filled the first few rows on the outdoor patio. I felt all eyes on me as I walked across the patio, which had been illuminated with candles and white Christmas lights. You had to give it to the Deltas. When they hosted an event, they did so with class. Even though their chapter was small, comprised of women from both Georgetown and nearby American University, they still gave every event all of their heart. Even at that second, several of them were scuttling around, ensuring that the microphones and speakers were working properly.

The freshman ladies were still staring at me, and I felt vaguely uncomfortable. I looked through them to find friends to sit with, but I saw no one. I stood for a minute and looked around me, taking in the ambiance of the evening.

"Adrian!" someone called.

It was Tasha, a friend of mine since the previous year. She was sitting on the opposite end of the patio, so I had to walk in front of the sea of freshmen women to sit with her. I inhaled, exhaled, and walked toward Tasha. I turned to the women and gave a half-smile. Blank stares were given in return.

"Damn, after all that, I still didn't even get a hello," I told Tasha as I pulled up a chair next to her.

"What are you bitchin' about now?" she asked.

"Them freshmen over there. All up in my face, and they still don't say 'hello.' Don't they know you got to speak at Georgetown University?" I complained.

"Adrian, calm down…they didn't get the memo yet. Plus, they probably just think you're cute," Tasha explained.

"Cute? Whatever," I said. I turned back to the girls and they appeared to be conversing with one another. Several still had their eyes on me as they compared notes. "Well, maybe so. But I don't like that shit."

"Adrian…" Tasha sighed. "You're so difficult." Tasha was another local girl. Folks from the DC area tended to get along really well with one another at Georgetown. Whether it meant taking over a party when go-go music comes on, or just sitting out on a bench and talking about people, we were a family, albeit a really small one. We needed each other, because even though we still went to school within the boundaries of the city we called home, we might as well have been a thousand miles away. We needed each other to lean on, to hang out with, and to speak our own dialect with. I was glad to have found Tasha; even though one of the many rumors spreading about either of us was that we were dating.

There was no denying it: Tasha was beautiful. She was slender and brown skinned, thick in all of the right places and nothing fake on her or about her. She had long black hair, which she usually just wore in a ponytail. Her eyes were dark brown, deep and entrancing. There's no doubt that if I weren't Adrian Collins, I would have tried to talk to Tasha seriously, especially since she was chronically single.

But I was Adrian Collins, and my interests laid elsewhere. On that night, my interest was in hearing some good poetry. I wasn't much of a writer myself, but I thoroughly enjoyed hearing the animated pieces that Georgetown's students were famous for. The average student was so wound up with stress that we didn't have any choice but to explode through poetry.

The Mistress of Ceremonies, a Senior Delta from American whom I had never met, quieted down the crowd and introduced the first poet. Tasha and I sat through several really good poets, but neither of us was truly impressed until the next to last poet got on the microphone.

"Ladies and gentlemen," the MC announced. "It is my honor to welcome back to the Crimson Cipher stage a poet who is near and dear to many of us at both Georgetown and American. I first met this poet when I was a sophomore, and I was blown away. For those of you who have never heard this gentleman before, you are in for a treat. Ladies and gentlemen, representing the class of '99-"

"Nine-Nine!" all of the seniors simultaneously interjected.

"Carlos Ortiz!"

Those who did not know Carlos politely applauded, and those who did screamed for him.

"Who is this guy?" I asked Tasha.

"I don't know," Tasha replied. "He must have been abroad last semester."

"Shh!" someone in the audience said.

Tasha and I rolled our eyes and focused on a legend that we knew nothing about.

"Hi everybody..." Carlos said politely. "Thanks for that warm welcome, and thanks to the Deltas for holding down this tradition over the years. Um, I see a lot of new faces out there, and I guess you all are like 'Who's this guy?' Well, my name is Carlos and the reason that you don't know me is because I was abroad all last year in Costa Rica, and then in Senegal. I guess tonight, I want to share an 'oldie-but-goodie' that a lot of the upperclassmen haven't heard for two years. This one is called 'Recognize.'"

Upon hearing the title of the poem, several girls a few seats down from Tasha and me cheered. They were Seniors, and obviously friends of Carlos.

The poet cleared his throat and began the poem, which had a fast and syncopated cadence. He said each vowel of each word with energy, as if the poem's success depended on the audience member not missing a single sound. His whole demeanor changed from mild-mannered to fiery, in the space of seconds.

It's something I should realize
It's nothing I can theorize
The prophecy is hard to see
It used to come so naturally
I'm writing a biography
Of two young people, you and me
It's plain to see
No fantasy
I mean that we

Should probably and naturally
Forget about the world you see
And magnify and beautify
A set of people, you and I
Secretly, I share my thoughts
Until your mind is at a loss
I'm so unkind, it blows your mind
All because of this phrase of mine
Would you like to
Play a little game with me
Or maybe read a book to me
You can see I'm your baby
Always, now, forever more
A secret's what will be in store
So recognize and realize
That I just can't apologize
For feeling freaky ways I feel
And knowing what I feel is real
That I just
Love me
Some you"

The audience erupted with applause upon the conclusion of the poem. Although we didn't know it, Carlos Ortiz was back and in full effect. My eyes followed him as he smiled, thanked the audience, and quickly took his seat.

I gave Tasha a sideways glance, which she returned. I smiled.

The evening ended with one more poet, whom I felt sorry had to follow Carlos. My mind was on the Latin poet until the MC announced where the after party was going to be. Of course Tasha and I would be there. Ever since we knew each other, we rarely turned down the opportunity to party for free on campus.

As the crowd began to leave the Cipher, I felt a tap on my shoulder.

"So what are you gonna do?" Tasha asked me.

"Watch this," I said.

I rose from my seat and made a beeline for Carlos Ortiz. This was one man that I at least had to meet. There was a crowd of mostly females around who seemed to know him. I stood off to the side, waiting to introduce myself to him.

One of the girls happened to turn around and notice me.

"Adrian! How are you?" she asked.

"I'm fine, Keisha, how are you?" I asked. She was Keisha Jones, a fellow board member of the NAACP.

"Fine. Hey, you don't know Carlos, do you?" Keisha asked me.

"I sure don't," I replied.

"Well, let me introduce you. Hey Carlos!" The young man stopped his conversation with a young lady and faced Keisha and me.

"What's up?" Carlos asked Keisha.

"This is Adrian Collins," Keisha said. "He is the Vice-President of the NAACP this year."

"Hi, Adrian…Carlos," he said. As he extended his hand, he flashed a brilliant smile that exposed two crooked teeth on the bottom.

"Nice meeting you," I said. "Excellent poetry, by the way."

"Thank you," he replied, never once dropping his smile. "What year are you?"

"Oh, I'm a Sophomore."

"And already the Vice-President of the NAACP? That's dope,"

"Thanks," I responded. Suddenly, I had nothing else to say. A nervous smile and a quickly beating heart replaced my usually witty repartee.

"Adrian…" Keisha added to the awkward silence. "Adrian is helping to reevaluate the program of the NAACP. In fact, you're planning a forum in a few weeks, right Adrian?"

"Oh yeah," I remembered. "We're holding a forum about black and Latino unity. We're gonna focus on mostly Georgetown and college campuses, but we're going to have some materials available about the history of Black and Brown relations."

"Word?" Carlos said. "That's tight, man. We definitely didn't have anything like that when before I went abroad."

"I know, right?" Keisha said. "That forum is all Adrian's idea, so it should be tight."

"Yeah," I said. "I'm enjoying planning it, but I hope we have enough participation."

"Oh, I wouldn't worry about that," Carlos said. "I'll definitely be there. And if you're as on point as Keisha is implying, then the people will support anything with your name on it."

"Wow…thanks," I said. I was definitely embarrassed now, for not only was Keisha giving me a lot of respect, so was Carlos, who had enough fans to be considered a celebrity in his own right. I started feeling a little self-conscious again, and I changed the subject.

"So, are y'all going to the after party?" I asked.

"Oh, yeah," Carlos said. "I haven't been to a party since I've been back. Where is it gonna be?"

"I think over in Henle," Keisha said.

"Cool," Carlos responded. "I'll see you there, right?" Carlos asked me.

"Oh, most definitely! I never miss a party," I said.

"Tight. I'll see you there," Carlos said.

"Bet," I responded. I told Keisha goodbye, and I turned to find Tasha again. She was where I left her, at her seat.

"So…?" she asked me.

"So…he'll be at the party tonight," I said. "Yo, man, he was giving me mad props."

"Word?" Tasha asked.

"Yeah, I mean Keisha was bigging me up, and he was chiming right in." I said.

"That's tight, man, do your thing," Tasha said.

"I'm trying, girl. I got to be me, and I got nothing to lose." I said. Tasha and I walked back to Tasha's room in Darnall Hall, which was located adjacent to Henle Village, where the party was to be held later on.

"So does this mean you're…you know," Tasha asked as we sat on the bed in her room.

"Naw, man. Not yet," I responded. "I'm just going to test the waters, do my thing. I'm still not trying to be the only one."

"I hear you, Adrian, but for real, how are you going to be able to tell?"

"I don't know," I said. "I mean, Carlos seems real cool, but it's gonna be a waiting game. I mean, we were flirting like a mug tonight, but you know how fucking stupid straight men are. You could have a hand on their crotch and a tongue in their ear and they still won't understand that you're trying to hit on them."

Tasha laughed. "That's true. I know you've been let down a lot."

"Yeah," I said. "Falling in love with straight men ain't cool."

"And you did a lot of that last year."

"Didn't I?" I said. I thought back to my freshman year, which had really only ended a few months before. I thought about the many men that I found attractive and had become close to, none of whom were gay. I got depressed, and that's one of the real reasons that I was so militant. Everything else was true, but I also just wasn't happy with my own identity yet.

"But things are different now," I said to Tasha. "I'm not sweating anybody. If Carlos is gay, so be it. If he's not, so be it. I'm not looking for a man, just somebody to kick it with."

"But that's what I'm asking," Tasha said. "How are you going to find somebody to kick it with if you aren't out of the closet?"

"I mean, it's not about wearing rainbows and pink triangles, yo," I explained. "That's not what I am, that's not what I'm about. I don't think you can look at me and tell that I'm gay, but at the same time, I wouldn't deny it if anyone asked me."

"Really?" Tasha asked. "So you're telling me that if one of those thugged out basketball players was to ask you, you'd say 'Yeah'?"

"I mean, maybe, depending on why they were asking…"

"Well, let me ask you this," Tasha began. "Why do you think Carlos might be gay?"

I thought about Tasha's question for a few moments. "Well," I began. "First of all, did you notice how his poem was mad ambiguous? No 'he's' or 'she's' at all. And the content was pretty vague, too. I mean, don't get me wrong, the poem was phat, but it wasn't the typical Georgetown "I-want-to-fuck-you-tonight" poem."

"Maybe that's because he's just a good poet," Tasha rebutted.

"True, that could be it," I said. "But it's also his look. His style, it's kind of trendy. Not really hip-hop or preppy. Almost like he gets all of his clothes from Urban Outfitters or something. But more than that, it was the actual interaction we had. The handshake lingered for just a second too long. He never stopped smiling."

"Yeah, I peeped that," Tasha said. "And you know what? Don't get gassed, but I did notice him and Keisha sort of giggling after you walked away."

"Good looking out," I said. "You know, it really seemed like Keisha was almost trying to set something up between us. Just a little."

"Did you ever tell her about you?" Tasha asked.

"Naw, man," I said. "I've only told a handful of people, and she wasn't one of them. In fact, I don't think any of the seniors know."

"Do you think she might assume that you are?"

"Maybe," I said. "I think people might assume that I am because I don't have a girlfriend and I'm not looking for one."

"Yeah, but there are still people who think we're together."

"Damn, can two people of opposite sexes just be friends?" I asked rhetorically.

"Apparently not at Georgetown..." Tasha answered.

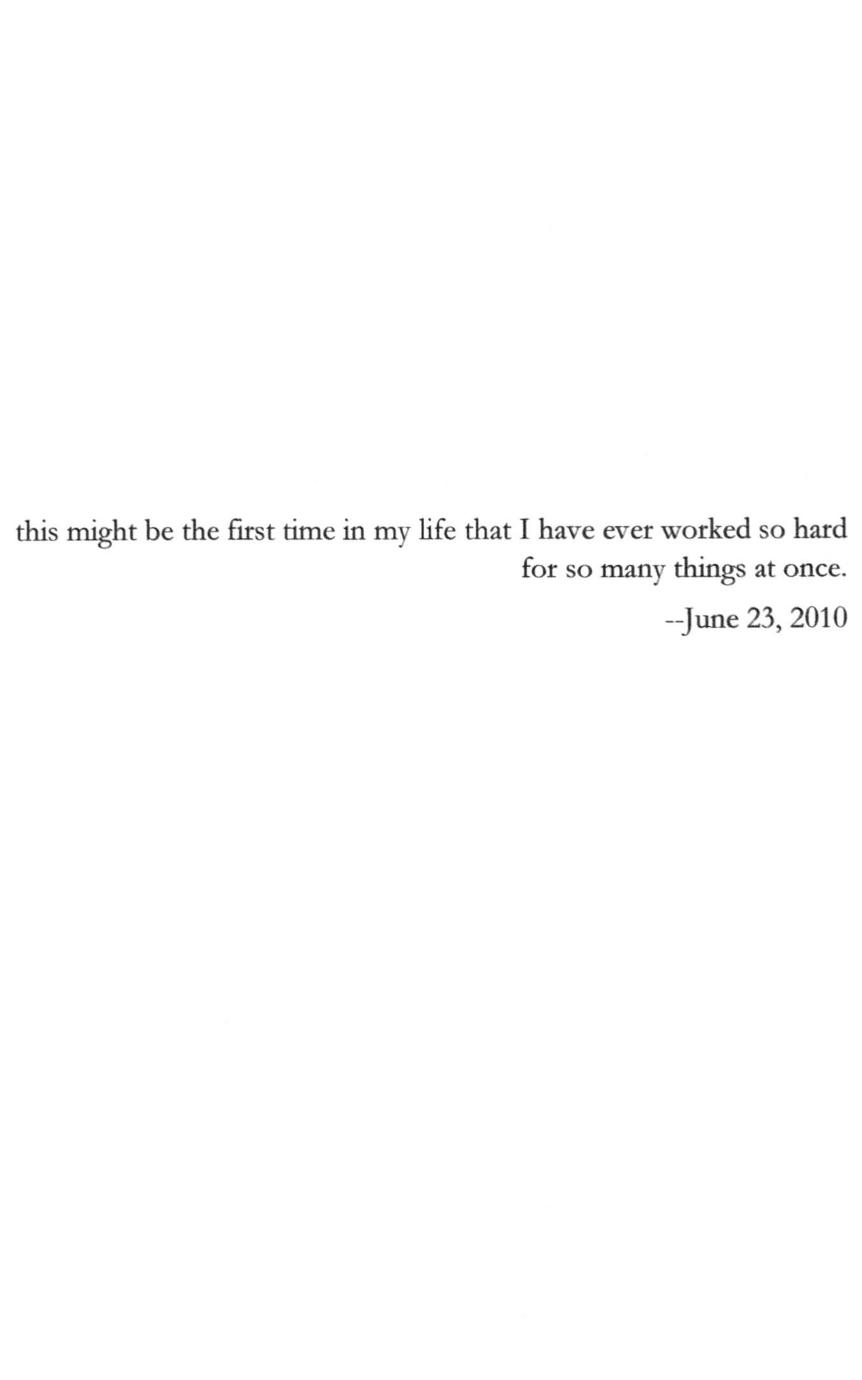

this might be the first time in my life that I have ever worked so hard for so many things at once.

--June 23, 2010

CHRISTMAS DREAM
2001

I am in an airport and I run into Tamera Ware, my line mate, who at first, I do not want to speak to. I am in the past. It is her first day of school—she is switching planes somewhere and she is on her way to school. She is preoccupied with herself, so I ignore her as well. She is talking to herself, to me really, loudly, as though I am supposed to be talking to her, so I do. Eight reddish brown spiders are creeping about a foot forward, then hop half a foot back, diagonally across the concrete. There is a ramp to bring wheeled carts of luggage up and down. It is not a lobby, but more like a baggage and freight area. Tamera then tells me about lice that I supposedly have in my hair from the airplane, about how many people sit in the seats before I ever get to the seats.

I go into the airport proper while Tamera figures out her flight situation. She has missed her connecting flight by five minutes, but before that, I have seen a line of planes take off one after the other, dangerously close, as a matter of fact. In the airport, I am trying to figure out my next flight and I have no ticket. I know I am approved for travel. All I need to do is figure out what the next plane is.

Marvin appears to help me. He seems to know which window to go to, which has no title. It is actually a window within a window. The man we are speaking to (German or Polish) is not even the correct man, as he is in the inner window. I ask him what flight I am supposed to be on, what time the next flight to Los Angeles is. He is silent. Marvin then takes what I presume to be an official request to know the information and fills it out, sliding it to the worker along with a five-dollar bill and repeating the question. The worker takes the money, which at this point I know is a bribe of some sort, but still fails to answer the question. I am discouraged that I still do not know what flight I am supposed to be on, but not scared that I can't get home. I say "well damn" or something and Marvin and I begin to walk away from the counter.

Suddenly, airport security comes out of nowhere, more German men, and they take Marvin and I into their custody. We are led to a staircase and I present my wrists to appear contrite and possibly be handcuffed. We are not handcuffed. The staircase has wood paneling and looks just like the staircase in my grandmother's basement. It *is* my grandmother's basement. We are led into her basement bathroom, which is now an interrogation room. Where the toilet was is now a regular chair of some sort. Or, it still could be a toilet, I really don't remember. At any rate, across from the toilet, mere inches, is a ledge, which curves in a U shape, and is thicker in the corners of the U than any place else. We are led to these seats, and the German general man sits on the toilet/chair. The second German officer closes the wood paneled door on us, and I am uncomfortable sitting furthest away from the door, facing the toilet and the wall to my right shoulder. I resist, and open the door, on the left side, just a crack. I tell them that it is because of the odor of the bathroom, but really it is because I am claustrophobic.

Marvin has said nothing, but I know that he and I are in the mess together. I can tell that he is extremely sad and hurt that he has put me in the situation, but he says nothing. The general asks him first what we thought we were doing, and I cannot remember the answer, or even if it was audible, but it was not satisfactory to the general. By the way, they all definitely had accents. The men also had bushy white mustaches and maybe even glasses or a monocle. The officer then asks me what happened, and I explain my side of the story, not really selling Marvin out, but explaining that I had never been in trouble like that before, and that I have the utmost respect for aviation and immigration laws, because at this point it seemed to be an immigration issue. It was definitely a federal issue, and even though our jailors were German, you can't tell me that this wasn't the United States.

After I gave my side of the story, it seems like a third German entered the bathroom, squeezing by the one who was at the door, and behind the one on the toilet/seat. The main German then asks what I want to be or do when I grow up. Did I want to be like they were, as supervisors and men of honor and action? Or did I want to be on the bottom scrubbing toilets? Because that's where hanging out with Marvin would take me, straight to the bottom.

I did not want our captors to know about me and Marvin, but I still wanted to comfort him because I knew what they said was hurtful to him. As the second general laughed in agreement, I touched Marvin on his leg, to psychically tell him "What they're saying isn't true," but he was non-responsive, as though he knew he had fucked up royally, and that I probably believed at least some of what the Germans were saying about him. They said additional mean things about Marvin being "scum" and again I tried to comfort him surreptitiously, but I dared not make eye contact. I noticed that Marvin's legs were thin as rails, and I could feel his knees hit one another.

It became clear that we were not being arrested, and were actually being released, but not after I smiled with the men and seemed to agree with them. However, I knew that I was only doing it so that Marvin and I could make a hasty exit from my grandmother's basement. I seem to remember picking Marvin up from his seat (which is interesting – I was sitting on the inside of the bathroom, but I picked him up from the outside) and leaving the bathroom and going into the laundry room. I cannot remember if Marvin ever got up from his seat.

Then, I heard someone counting down from seven and I saw an image of a digital display of red numbers, also counting down from seven. I cannot remember if the accompanying voice is that of a woman or of David Bowie. At zero, I could hear an alarm go off, and my body shook with each screech of the alarm, as if someone was having sex with me.

My world changed, and I was now floating above a kitchen table, hovering over a man who was fully clothed, who was humping a woman, who also seemed to be clothed. I can assume that he was penetrating her. The woman actually looked dead, her eyes were light and unblinking, her brown hair was fanned around her head, and her lips appeared to be blue. The man got up and the woman did not move. The woman disappeared, and the kitchen seemed to be a set for a Bowie video. The kitchen actually looked like the kitchen from "We Didn't Start the Fire." Marvin, the airport, the Germans were all gone. All that was left were what seemed to be evaluations of something, on yellow grids such as the ones given for standardized tests. And then I woke up.

LETTER TO FATHER

February 10, 2002

Dear Father,

I turn 23 years old this year, and I find out in a week whether I made it into American University's graduate program in Creative Writing. I got my undergraduate degree from Georgetown last May, and now I'm just working to bide my time until grad school. I'm also completing my first novel, which I am sure will end up selling well. I have a lot of good friends in my life, and we all remained close after we graduated, both physically and in spirit.

I'm not asking you for anything, really. I'm too old for child support or help paying the four years of tuition, room, and board for Georgetown. I have a great life. Anything I want, I can go out there and earn. There are only three things I need right now to complete my life:

1) A relationship with my father, no matter how screwed up it might be. Most men my age can say they love or hate their fathers. Give me the respect of at least knowing you.

2) A relationship with my siblings, because no matter how close my friends may be, I still deserve to look up to my older brother, and protect my younger sister, whose name I don't even know.

3) A relationship with my grandparents. When I called my grandmother when I was in high school, she did not know who I was. That's cool, I think it's kinda swell that I was the family secret. But your sister had no right to tell me not to call my own grandmother anymore. Your sister has nothing to do with the relationship you and I have.

If nothing else, respect me enough as a man to contact me with the answers I need. My email address is… My cell is…

And if you don't believe that I am your son, we can always arrange a blood test to get a definitive answer. This is not a game to me. I have a right to know my own heritage.

Sincerely,
Rashid

SOMETIMES WHEN THE MOON WAXES

FEBRUARY 15, 2002

sometimes when the moon waxes (or wanes) and i feel those pains winding through my mind. . .i can never figure out if its waxing and waning or if my mind is straining at the seams to leap out, if you know what I mean
moonbeams caressing my sol. or soul, i can never tell which one it is, either waxing or waning or the pain that is straining. . .the sun reflects off the disc and it still hurts my eyes, a reflection of a seduction of the world of the living that i am fiending for
walking in the dark -- dead -- walking in the graveyard of intellectual contemporaries -- dead, street hustlers and preachers, and pimps -- dead -- not knowing whether to praise god or the dollar down in the country holler
tick
dollar
tock
holler
the stars shine so bright
so bright
that you can't sleep at night, and then i closed my eyes

LOOKING FOR NELL CARTER

White boys are so pretty/Skin as smooth as milk
White boys are so pretty/Hair like Chinese silk

So last night, I was watching/listening to one of my favorite musicals of all time, *Hair*. I used to have a VHS tape of *Hair* from when it was on the A&E channel this one time. I swear I wore that tape out from fast forwarding through the commercials and watching it over and over again.

Luckily, I got a DVD player and sometime last year finally got *Hair* on DVD. It's one of the DVDs I will pop in and listen to while I am trying to get other work done. You know…for noise effect, as they say.

But this time was a little different. It felt like the movie was speeding along. Next thing I knew we were at the scene at the draft board and the musical number "Black Boys." Intercut with scenes of the naked white boy and the black members of the draft board were shots of three black women in central park, ogling and cat-calling the white boys there. One of those three black women was a slimmer (but still thick) Nell Carter. I couldn't turn my head as she sang the opening lines of the song:

White boys are so sexy
Legs so long and lean

At this point she grabs her thigh and looks at the white boys like "oops!" It is one of the best moments in the entire movie for me.

Love those sprayed-on trousers
Love the love machine

And she does this bump and it's just like *ah man, that is one sexy woman.* She owned her sexuality – I don't think I knew what it meant to own your sexuality until that moment. No, she wasn't perfect – she was short and always had a weight problem, but in 1979, this was just a little thick woman who was so confident, so beautiful…

Most people from my generation know Nell Carter from the show *Gimme a Break!* And that's cool, *Gimme a Break!* was a great show. At the time, I think black folks may have been up in arms about this fantabulous Broadway actress with the full, rich voice portraying, of all things, a maid. I'm sure people were like damn…again? Why must we always be servants to white folks, even when we're the star of the show?

But Nell wasn't a maid.

As a kid in Kindergarten, I didn't see race. In fact, when my mom asked me "What color is your teacher?" I said "Oh, she's about your color." So I didn't see a modern-day "Mammy." I saw a lady who took care of her friend's husband and children after she died. (People were sho nuff dying all the time in 80's sitcoms, weren't they?)

Though the "sassy housekeeper with a heart of gold" archetype had been done before (and still is done), Nell Carter brought to the role confidence and sexuality. Maybe I am remembering this wrong, but didn't she always have a thing for Billie Dee Williams on the show? She was never androgenized or desexualized like Paula Kelly or Marsha Warfield on *Night Court*, nor was she made into a vamp like Jackée on *227*. She was in many ways just an average single woman.

Almost all of my favorite moments from *Gimme a Break!* involved her singing. Damn, her voice was beautiful – is there a Nell Carter album somewhere? Gotta be. Anyway, I remember this one time that she sat in front of the piano and started singing "Memory" from *Cats*.

Memory…
All alone in the moonlight
I remember the old days
I was beauuuutiful thennnnn….

She was such a ham – I loved it!

Then of course the men who were always trying to marry her. Remember: "This is the church, this is the steeple, open it up and here are all the people waiting for us to get married, Nell!"

And how about when Nell and Addie (Telma Hopkins) went to

Mississippi (or Alabama?) to visit Nell's sister, who for some reason, always had beef with her. What finally brought them together was when they played some old records and started singing along. It seemed so natural, like they were really all best friends.

Then of course the show jumped the shark when they went to New York. It was still good to me (I was in elementary school; nothing really sucked about television), but it was eventually cancelled.

Nell Carter also appeared on *Hangin' With Mr. Cooper* and Reba after *Gimme a Break*. Before that, she appeared in *Hair*, *Ain't Misbehavin'* (on and off-Broadway as well as a television version), and later a 20th Anniversary revival of *Annie*.

On Thursday, January 23, 2003, we got the news:

> *BEVERLY HILLS, California (CNN) -- Actress and singer Nell Carter, best known for her role as the housekeeper in the TV sitcom "Gimme a Break!", died Thursday. She was 54.*
>
> *Carter's publicist Roger Lane said Carter collapsed and died of natural causes in her Beverly Hills home.*
>
> *She had suffered from diabetes and had recovered from a near-deadly bout with a brain aneurysm in the 1990s. Lane said he did not know if her diabetes contributed to her death.*

I think I was pretty hurt by it, as much as I would be by any actor dying before their prime, but especially one I had grown up watching nearly every day in syndication.

I didn't find out until months later that Nell Carter loved women the same way that I love men. Damn you, *E! True Hollywood Stories.*

I remember watching it with my mom and in the very last thirty seconds of the program, they said almost verbatim what you can find on the internet now:

> *When she died, friends and family were surprised to discover barely $200 in her bank account. They were further startled to discover that Carter had been living as a closeted lesbian, and that custody of her children had been left to her domestic partner.*

My mouth fell open and my mom said "Uh-huh! Betcha didn't know THAT one, didya?!"

I wish that I had always known that Nell Carter loved women. Yes, she had been married at one point. But I don't know...did she really ever love men? Did she always love women? Was she on the "DL?"

I hate that I'll never know the answers to these questions.

It's like maybe in my subconscious mind, I always knew that she was one of us, no matter how many men proposed to the *Gimme a Break!* Nell, no matter how many white men she cat-called in *Hair.* She owned her sexuality on stage and in private. She lived with her woman at the end of her life. The custody of her children went to her partner. That's love.

I want to meet Nell Carter. I want to know if she identified as a black Lesbian. I want to give her a hug. I want to help her manage her money better and get good health insurance and help her keep her weight off. I would stop her from eating those "funeral foods" that are killing black folks.

But she's gone and been gone.

I don't want to lose any more of my heroes and sheroes. I want all gay black people to live to be a hundred, or however long it takes for them to come out. I don't want one of my heroes to be outed by *E!* I want them to come out on their own terms, to be the role models, to be proactive. I want them to stand with me for equal marriage rights. I want them to fight AIDS with me.

I want them to stand up as proud men who love men, women who love women, and whoever loving whomever. I don't want Keith Boykin to do this alone. We need our activists, yes, but we need our actors, lawyers, doctors, singers, writers, filmmakers, rappers (yes, rappers), teachers, politicians – we need you out *here.* Not in the closet.

Some pebbles in the pond cause ripples. Some cause tidal waves. Imagine what this world would be like if people could really be themselves? We would actually see the diversity that exists among all people, straight or gay.

And maybe one day, nobody will care anymore. And then we will have won.

See you on the other side, Ms. Carter.

DIARYLAND

2003-07-09 | 9:27 p.m.

i really am a fucking basket case
and i feel sorry for whoever
falls in love with me.
if THAT ever happens.

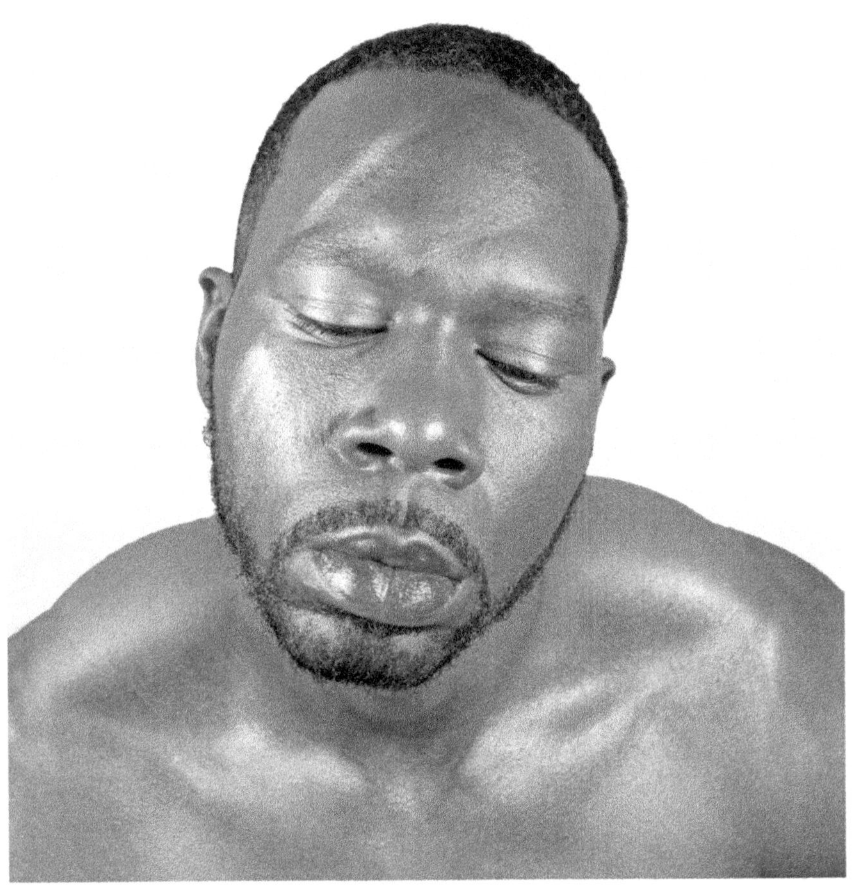

PEACE BE

August 20, 2003

i write the silence
for the sound holds my pen still

peace be

i write the silence of a man who cannot legally love
but can legally vote for the man who stole florida
and can legally die for the men who stole obatala's children
and can legally drag a puff of the magic stick
shorty, if you get hit once, you can't die twice

peace be

i write the silence of a son of a silent age
a boy who cannot tell his mama
a scared little boy
i write the silence of a chosen son
chosen, but not chose;
not loved

peace be

i write the silence of the age of free love
free at a cost
freedom for you, but not for me
i am not free to love
peace be
peace be

the sound holds my pen still because i hear the
screams of pink triangles at
bergen-belsen
and
bayard rustin held my hand as i cried

and
james baldwin held my dreads back
as i puked
the revelation manifesting itself in
the pit of my stomach

"your faggot ass ain't free, nigger"

peace be

considering i have no idea what's after this,
i am gonna go ahead and love the hell out of being alive

--July 4, 2010

I AM A TEACHER

December 1, 2003

I am a teacher.
Oh…My…God.

How did I get myself into this? I thought to myself nearly every day that I taught at Jessie LaSalle Elementary School in Northeast Washington. I knew exactly how I got myself in that situation, though.

Six months prior to taking the job at LaSalle, I was a volunteer at Calvin Coolidge High School. I worked wherever they needed me – with gifted kids in the Advanced Placement English class, grading book reports for Biology I, and helping developing readers with their college essays. Somewhere along the line, I thought to myself "Hey…I can do this." I quickly signed up for my substitute teacher credentials, for if I was to really know whether or not I wanted to be a professional teacher, I needed more time in the classroom.

I got my first sub assignment in September with Second Graders. I received a lot of help from a teacher named Mrs. Sizer. Her actual title was Intermediate Coach, which means she helped coordinate planning, staff development, classroom management, and general assistance with the intermediate grades. She was a big help in getting me to learn things I take for granted, such as how to take students to the lavatory.

The school secretary told me that they would need a long-term substitute for a woman going on maternity leave. I said that I would definitely consider it.

I had a friend who died in a car accident this summer. I wasn't even sure if returning to American was the best thing for me, but I needed something to do – something to feel dedicated to. My friend was a faithful member of Teach for America. I never applied for TFA, mostly because I knew how competitive it was, and I had seen friends of mine rejected, even with better GPAs and more activities than me. So when the opportunity arose for me to teach, like she had, I took it.

At the end of my first day as a sub, I was offered the long-term sub position for the sixth-grade class. Actually, I was thrust into it. I attended a staff meeting, where the Principal announced that I would be taking over the class.

Thanks for asking me if I felt ready for such a task, Mr. Crocker!

I took the job because I knew I was needed, and the school felt that I was ready. By the end of my experience, I learned that even the most well-prepared teachers are never ready for that first day, week, month, or year in the classroom.

My strength was discipline. Sometimes, simply being a man helped. Most of the boys looked to me as a big brother figure, someone they really did not want to disappoint or feel the proverbial wrath. This relationship did not happen overnight, though. The majority of my class was just bad. Most education professionals are loathe to call kids bad. Well, these professionals had never been with the 22 sixth graders in Mr. Darden's class. Bad, I tell you. But highly entertaining.

The first week or two was really all about establishing my presence and authority. The teacher on maternity leave had left unexpectedly early, and really did not have a substitute folder which matched up with what the students were actually learning at the time. We persevered anyway, though. My goal was the have the kids do the work that was assigned to them…quietly. They had to respect themselves, each other, and me as their teacher.

It was hard, but I never gave up, nor did I want to. Leaving that assignment was never an option for me. I knew that I would never be the type of teacher that the others in the school were, but I did think that I could be the best possible sub I could be. If nothing else, we could all at least follow a schedule.

That is, if I could get their behavior under control.

I had one student, Lorenzo. He was one of the best math students in the school. I, on the other hand, still struggle with long division. Lorenzo was the type of student that one might call a "ringleader." None of the other boys in the class would act up if Lorenzo told them not to. But if Lorenzo himself was being disrespectful, you can believe that they all would follow suit.

So how could I deal with Lorenzo? Well, I knew that Lorenzo was smart – smarter than his classmates. I do not mean this in a disparaging way. It's just that Lorenzo was slick. He knew how to irritate his classmates and goad them into behaving badly, all the while getting his work done on time, and correctly. I had to figure out a way to keep Lorenzo busy with his schoolwork while not distracting others.

Well, I devised something in my class called a "speaker's list" and tested it out on Lorenzo. When it was time for group reading, instead of stopping each student after they had read a few paragraphs, I decided to modify what I had learned in my own years in Model UN. I told Lorenzo that he would be in charge of creating and managing a speakers list of all the students who wanted to read selections of a story. Lorenzo was allowed to call on students and place them in order on the blackboard. Lorenzo instinctively knew how to be fair – he almost always alternated boy readers with girl readers. He also determined for how long someone would read aloud. If the reader was not strong, he would not let them belabor themselves for too long.

Somehow, I found the answer. Lorenzo loved responsibility, and it kept him in line. From that moment on, Lorenzo had more respect for me as his teacher, could demonstrate respect for his student by helping them learn and not distracting them, and maybe even picked up some self-esteem through his leadership.

As I said, my strength was discipline. Some substitute teachers left Ms. Clark's class and told the school that they would never take that class again. I didn't see it. Sure, my kids misbehaved. And yes, they were probably the worst behaved in the school. But it just didn't faze me like it fazed other teachers.

My students had problems turning in their homework. Rather than berate them, they had to write down their excuse why they hadn't done their homework, and their parent had to sign it. When a student or group of students misbehaved, they would have to write sentences – long sentences. I called parents frequently. I changed seating arrangements whenever I needed to. Some students even had to write essays on respect that their parents had to sign.

In addition to punishment, I took great pleasure in positive reinforcement and incentives. As a teacher, the dollar store is your friend. I was able to pick up trinkets and toys to give out as small "surprise, you were good today" gifts. I also found a stash of "Good Job!" certificates that the permanent teacher had left in a drawer. I could notice the changes in the students who received these incentives. They were inspired to keep up their good work. Those who might have missed out on that day made improvements as well. They knew that they were *good* students. They just made the wrong choices sometimes.

Once the students saw that I was serious, and that I would be on board until at least January, they settled down. Now I had to make the transition from disciplinarian and conveyor of busy work to an actual educator. I had to learn how to manage my classroom, how to maintain a grade book, and how to assist those students on Individualized Educational Plans. I met with Mrs. Sizer and Mrs. Hamilton, the other sixth grade teacher. I was introduced to pacing charts, which taught me that sometimes students don't start at chapter one in a textbook.

It was all so new to me. I had no idea how time-consuming elementary education really was. I hung in there, though. My students were learning, and I was learning my students. I learned that just because a student is in special education doesn't mean that they are slow in all subjects. I had one student, Britteny, who needed extra help in math, but was a great writer. I also learned that special education and behavior problems are not necessarily related. One special ed student, Rondell, was quite a handful. But another, Mahmood, never gave me any problems whatsoever. I could tell that Mahmood viewed me more as a big brother figure. He did his best not to disappoint me and felt genuinely guilty when I caught him acting up.

I had my humorous moments in the class, as well. Being a disciplinarian was tough! There were moments when some of the wittier students knew exactly when to try and make me laugh. There was one moment when a normally quiet student, Yemi, made an uncharacteristic outburst. We're not talking a slight yell here. Yemi turned into the Incredible Hulk on us and screamed to his unwitting victim "I HATE YOU!" I quickly told him to step into the hallway and calm down.

Of course, the class was already in stitches because of Yemi's behavior, but I tried to keep my game face on. Unfortunately, the absurdity of the situation replayed itself in my mind again and again. I was thinking to myself "Wow, he really just 'hulked out' on us."

The smile started in the corner of my mouth, and I turned my head while telling the students to stop laughing. I couldn't let them see me smile!

"Mr. Darden's about to laugh, y'all," one student said. "Look at him!"

"No, I'm not," I said, now totally facing the opposite direction of the class.

"He 'bout to laugh! Mr. Darden is laughing!"

"Shut up!" I said, the tears now streaming from my face. I sat down at my desk.

"Mr. Darden," one student began, "Are we gonna have to send you to the principal's office?"

I lost it. I was now laughing. Of course, this was the first time I have "broken" in front of the students, so they were highly entertained by seeing me laugh so hard. Luckily, we all calmed down long enough for me to go speak to Yemi seriously in the hallway, and bring him back again, none the wiser.

I was taken off of my long-term assignment because I came down with bronchitis and couldn't work. I will be honest and say that I felt betrayed. LaSalle had invested time and energy into training me. They had taken a risk on me, and I felt that it was paying off. The students were learning. Their behavior was improving. Parents were becoming more active. I felt that I couldn't control being sick, so couldn't we make some sort of Plan B?

The longer that I was sick, the less likely a Plan B seemed possible.

I think that overall, my experience was a positive one for me and the students. I learned a lot from all the teachers who I had a chance to observe.

My one complaint or regret is that when I was taken off the assignment, no one told the students why. No one explained to them "Mr. Darden is too sick to work." No one explained to them that I didn't abandon them, like too many of them had already been abandoned by the men in their lives. I felt pretty disappointed in that, especially since I felt a certain kinship with the principal as a fellow black man.

I have been well enough to work now for about a week. I have run into my former students, who all beg for me to come back. Mrs.

Sizer is now their full-time teacher, and Mr. Crocker, the principal, comes in to teach math and science. I know that they are learning a lot more than when I was their teacher – I can concede that fact.

But I can't help but feel a twinge of sadness when I hear the students being yelled at so loudly, that I have to close the door of the class I am covering.

Everything happens for a reason. I came into those students' lives to have some sort of impact on them, possibly an impact I may never personally see. Hopefully, when I am wandering about Riggs Plaza, I will run into them, and they will still have the same enthusiasm about life as they did when I had them for those few weeks in the Fall of 2003.

LETTER TO MARVIN

December 9, 2003

Dear Marvin,

So I was watching *The Cosby Show* on Nick at Nite last night. It was the episode where Denise goes off to college and Claire first starts berating Cliff about his eating habits. Claire, who I think everyone wishes was their mother at some point in their lives, said to Denise "I'm going to miss you. Not because I love you…but because I like you."

That was one of the most profound statements I've heard on television, and I really hope that I have kids who I can say that too one day. It's like you have to love your kids, but you're really blessed if you can say that you like your kids, too.

I'm too damn sentimental for my own good.

Marvin, I feel like my life is moving along fine. On one hand, my years since graduation have been filled with baby steps and setbacks. I worked in alumni relations and development for nine months and then quit. I took time off to do nothing but write. Then I did grad school. Shouldn't have gone back for a second year, but I did. And now I am quitting that. More time off to get some ventures off the ground and focus on finding that damn agent. And next…grad school at Howard for two years.

Maya died; my grandparents are both basically dying before my eyes. Grandpa has been in a home going on two years now, and my grandmother just had a recurrence of her cancer. Things aren't great…

But…things could be so much worse. I am so grateful for my four years at Georgetown because they brought so much to me. Directly and indirectly. The people who came into my life, whether they breezed through or came to stay. The lessons I learned….

I tell you, my mom says (jokingly) that Georgetown made me into a bigger asshole than I already was. HA! I don't know where I got it from, but I do think that I learned in undergrad how to get what I want, when I want it. I never saw Georgetown as one of those elitist schools. But I can't deny that any and all business sense I picked up was from just being a student there.

Which is exactly why I didn't last at American. At Georgetown, everyone worked with you for *your* goal. At American, every single person was an obstacle, a stopping point. It sucked man. How could I come to respect a community of artists when they wouldn't let me be who I am?

With all due respect to AU, I think it's a pretty good undergrad institution. But I would never encourage someone to go there for grad school. I know this guy in the dance program there who hates it as well. It seems that your prophecy came true. Well, it wasn't really a prophecy, more of a joke. Something about a school being named after the biggest fuck-up in world history. So true…so true!

I said in my email to you that I would be doing some different things in '04. Well, in addition to grad school in the Fall (hopefully) I will kick off a series of activities in the Spring.

First of all, I need to make some loot. But, after having taught, I know that the classroom is where I need to be. Teaching, or something. Helping others. So, I plan on opening an editing and proofreading business geared towards college and grad school students, for both academic essays and things like creative writing portfolios. I'll open up a website, a PayPal account, make some fliers, send out some emails…and maybe the dough won't exactly roll in, but it is something that could definitely take off if I market it correctly.

I will also be tutoring this kid around my way on Saturdays. He was one of my students, and I feel like I owe him something, after I was "fired" from my assignment for being sick. He is special ed and reads on the second-grade level, but I really feel like if I cooperate with his mom and the faculty, we can really change him around. He's not a *bad* kid, he just needs a whole lot of help. And possibly a big brother figure.

I'm at that age where I am not sure if I want to be a big brother or a dad, you know? I have this desire to take care of people, I guess. Maybe I don't really want to be a dad, cuz i ain't got no real job, hahaha. But I do want to be part of this community and show people that you can step up the game a notch and still be "of" the community. I don't think the boy will be a Rhodes Scholar. But maybe we can get him to a point where he can at least decide what he wants by the 12th grade, and not have it decided for him.

I will also make sure I can substitute at several other schools in this area. My high school is two short bus rides away, and it is across from an elementary school. I need money, dawg…and quitting grad school definitely hampers my abilities. No more refund check. Sigh. Tear.

But I will still see what I can do about coming to Thailand. It's not exactly on the "highly likely" side of the spectrum, but we'll see. If I get another long-term substituting gig, then the deal is sealed.

And who knows…I might have a contract. Wouldn't that be tight, Marvin? I have sent materials off to an agent who seems interested in the novel. She is the former agent of a published fraternity brother. He actually put me in contact with her. What luck! The same audience who bought his book is the same audience I want to buy mine. I am hoping, praying that she will like it, love it, want to represent me, and know precisely the publisher for me; I am also hoping they will want to edit it only slightly, and put me on the shelves as soon as possible.

From there, since we know how small publicity budgets are for new authors, we will launch a guerilla marketing assault. Emails, websites, fliers at barber shops and beauty salons…I have thought about this so long, Marvin. It's so much more than a dream. I am prepared to do what it takes to get this book on shelves and to make people love it.

It helps that I'm not a horrible writer. he he. I do know that I am not the best writer who ever lived. But I see the stuff that's out there, especially black fiction, and i am like "Dude! If they can be published, i KNOW i can!"

And really, the subject matter of my first few books is so different than what I really want to write as I get older. Speculative fiction…Octavia. God, love her!

Speaking of which…a long time ago, I told you about a black vampire story i was trying to write. Well, write before (or during) when i got sick, I started working on a serialized novella utilizing those ideas. It was/is to be a 12-part series of short stories. Like, almost like short-shorts. My plan was to write all twelve stories and then email them out to all my friends every few days. Get people hooked, like a soap opera.

It was/is really just a marketing plan to get my name out there into cyber space so that when my novel ultimately drops, people will be like, oh THAT guy! He's good!

It's a tactic I learned from Zane, the black female erotica writer. It kills two birds with one stone – I get to write, and I get to establish a fan base.

Somehow, I dropped the ball on that idea. I will pick it up again at some point, hopefully this spring when all of my other ideas get set into motion.

I felt we needed a pause in this letter because as you can see, my mind runs a mile a minute sometimes. I have problems setting plans into motion though. I think that I get discouraged by little things and then retreat into myself, if that makes sense. Like, when I got sick was a PRIME time for me to be writing. But I didn't for some reason. I would sit in front of the computer, and just feel like blah.

And I haven't read a novel in eons! I claim to be a fiction writer, but I don't find much enjoyment in novels anymore. I start, get bored, and stop.

But anyway…you might be wondering what I do when not cooped up in the room with the peeling wallpaper and water-damaged ceiling.

(Side note, the ceiling DID indeed start dripping one night, and nearly onto my head, but it missed me by six or seven inches. The roof was finally repaired, and it no longer leaks, though we need to still repaint the ceiling.)

Well, I hung out with Claudine during homecoming, and it seems like I hung out with Nikki…oh yeah, she took me to the clinic. Ha! I could barely talk that day, but she was right there for me. Love her!

I went to chapter meeting last month but skipped this month. (A first!) I really enjoy my chapter meetings usually. They are social to me…I get to meet all these older black men who just love seeing some young energy in the chapter. We also eat afterwards in the church basement where we meet.

Oh yeah! My friend Thomas (known as Tommy in high school, but he's too grown for that now) came over last week to hang out for a few hours. He didn't stay terribly long because well, he had to go screw his woman later on that evening. But this is one of the friends I told you that I really needed to connect with again. We did, and I'm glad. He is a character, Marvin. He'd like you, but I don't know how much you'd like him. Well, I'm sure you would like him.

He told me last weekend that he was "mad at me about the whole gay thing." I am like Thomas, why? He goes into this long story about this youth program we were in where I said that some girl was hot, and because I had "claimed" her, he couldn't pursue her. And now, I'm gay, so I basically cock-blocked him inadvertently. We had a good laugh about that one.

What is also funny…there are a good amount of gay men in my chapter, but I don't really like them very much. They are nice, but nosy. Well, the latest joke/rumor/assumption is that I am dating the chapter secretary, who is my very heterosexual FRIEND Sadat. Good heavens, can't a gay man have straight male friends nowadays? Sadat lives right around the corner and gives me rides to meetings, that's all. Damn gossipy queens.

Now for the sappy parts.

I LOVE YOU!!!! Loving you makes me feel free. I can't even explain that statement, but it's true. Not a day goes by that I don't think of you, Marvin. Believe it.

--Rashid

WHAT DO I WANT?

November 7, 2004

I want to be published. I want to have written a novel, or even several novels, for the sheer satisfaction of being published. Inside me, as in every artist, I just want my work to be available to the public. I do not want to have to go into debt to see this happen. Breaking even will be fine for me as long as I know I did my absolute best to make sure the "right" people have access to the work.

I want those who purchase the book to be incredibly happy that they did. I want all who read the book to believe that it is so good that I am selling it at too low a price. I want people who don't know me to feel proud that they supported an up-and-coming author.

I want my books to be vehicles for social change. I believe that I have a purpose for being on this earth, and that part of that purpose is to change people's lives in some way. I believe that my own novels will be vehicles for change. I want to produce positive, but authentic representations of gay African American men, to combat the negative stereotypes associated with black gay men, especially in the face of the "Down Low" hysteria.

I realize that this project is an ambitious one. I know that I do not have the money to do it on my own. I wish that I was independently wealthy. I wish that I had a great job that allowed me to take a few months to save up and do the damn thing. But I don't, and I am okay with that. I realize that the sacrifices I am making in my life now will pay off later. There is no other time in my life where I have had the flexibility to take time off just to write. The pay isn't great and there are no benefits, but I get to plan…I get to decide how my life could be.

I am fully aware that the first book is an investment, not a salary. I will not become rich or "paid" off of this book. My intent is to launch my career from the bottom up. I spent nearly two years searching for agents, and most said that though my writing was good, there was no room for me in the market, or that my writing was good, but they just didn't feel they had the contacts to help me.

Well…if agents don't have the contacts to get me into a major house, then I'll just have to turn it over to the people who really matter: the readers. People *love* to read. Who is an agent or an editor at a major house to decide what will and won't really sell? Yeah, yeah, I know – they get paid to ultimately sell books, so there is some truth to what they are saying about the market being oversaturated with "black authors."

But guess what? These people don't get paid to take risks. And I am a risk. I have written a novel about a gay man who pledges a black fraternity – one of the last taboos in my culture. It is a risk. I have thought time and again "what if I really don't have what it takes to tell this story?"

But I do. This process forces you to have self-confidence, or else you will fall by the wayside. I have one hundred percent faith that everyone who reads my novel will love it. I believe in the power of the "fan." If…when this book is a success, proven by empty book boxes in my basement, agents and publishers will take note that yes, this is what the public wants. If this thousand, three thousand, five thousand–whoever–if they love this novel and prove it by sending in testimonials to the website, then publishers will have no choice but to give me a second chance.

I know that I can do this. I have faith in my work. I pray to God so much, just thanking him for my talents. I know that if I wasn't a writer, I would be stuck at some job doing something I don't like working for and with people I don't care about.

My time is limited. I have about ten months before publication date, six months before I actually get the books from the printer, and just four months before the money needs to be raised, either in presales, donations, sponsorships, or a combination of them all. So basically, I need to start the presale in two months! But I can do this! I have always done my best work with tight deadlines.

I can do this. I can do this. I can do this.

I need to tailor a financing plan and promotional plan to suit my needs. My objective is not to make this a runaway success, but to produce a quality product that creates a fan base and starts a buzz among both the average reader and the people who "count."

God be with me. I need Him now more than ever.

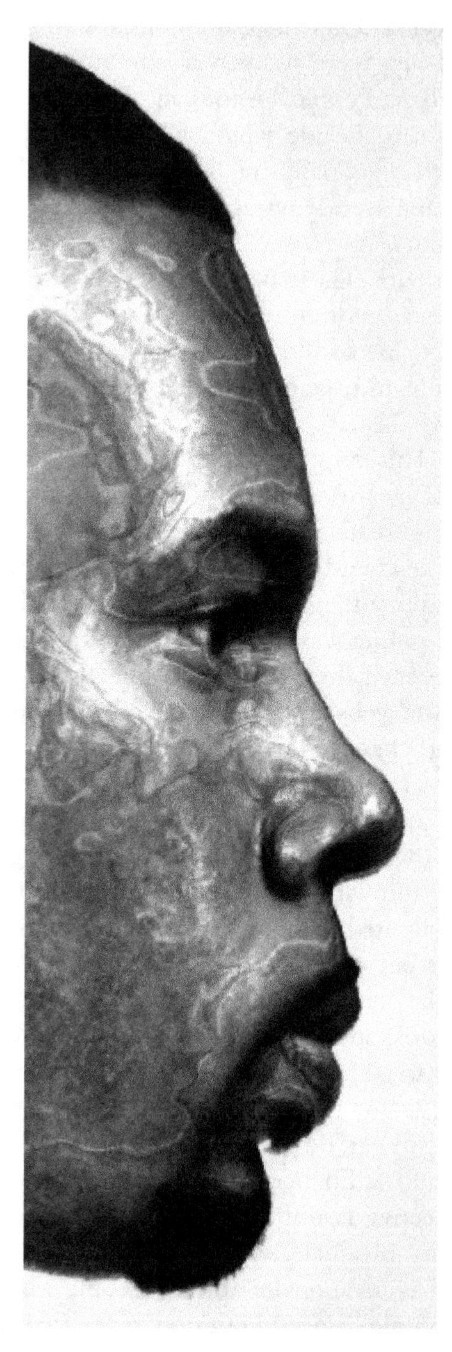

THE RED AND BLACK JOURNAL

May 2, 2006

I am probably too tired to adequately capture everything—plus, this pen ain't shit. And I'm funny about my pens.

But this journal will be about my passions…my lusts…my crushes…my anger.

These are the things I cannot talk about. Not out loud, not in my blog.

May 3, 2006—Morning

I am so extra sometimes. My emotionalism is usually warranted, but re-reading my own words sometimes is just ridiculous.

The last significant prose journal that I kept was during my freshman year in college. My passion in those days was Omega Psi Phi.

Nine years later, things have changed. I am an Alpha. Not to mention a gainfully employed college graduate.

On the other hand, other things haven't changed at all. Fundamentally, I still find myself attracted to inaccessible men.

Luckily, I can just laugh off my sexual attraction to straight men. Joke about it with the girls. Jack off and allow a brief image of those guys to cross my mind. But then it's over.

Making friends isn't a challenge for me. In fact, I value the relationships I have with straight men. Among all of my friendships, they feel most intimate.

So it stands to reason that I would—at least sometimes—become attracted to the very men that I befriend, knowing all along that they don't love other men the way that I do.

I hesitate to say that I "fall" for them—it's that if ever their orientation flipped, I'd happily pursue them. Not sexually, but romantically.

I would write more, but I'm at work now.

May 3, 2006—Early evening

I really do enjoy being a Site Director. I love the responsibility. I'm not yet drunk with power, but I'm damn near.

I think the principal here might be gay. No particular reason. When I first met him, I got that vibe.

He's very slender. I guess he's handsome. When I first met him, I emailed Dwayne and said he could "get it."

In retrospect, I don't think he could. His handsomeness wore off when I became acquainted with his leadership style. Plus, he's a little too skinny. PLUS, he pledged Sigma Chi! I felt like I had him all figured out when I learned he was in a "white" frat.

Like most men, I think I can determine the people I would sleep with within the first five minutes [of meeting them]. Okay, so make that one minute. And a week to decide if I would spend the rest of my life with them.

It's sad that I am only half joking.

As I write in this journal, the major themes will probably tie into falling for men too hard and too fast; past "loves," and loneliness. And a whole lot of lust and longing.

Yes, I miss [Spencer] a whole lot somedays, but I don't let myself think about him for too long.

Later, on the bus.

Life is good.

I didn't have to expel any kids.

I really like my [Test Literacy Instructors].

The two things I need to work on:

- Efficiency with paperwork
- Relationship with "Mod Squad"

Paperwork…attendance is under control. I enter it daily the next morning at the office. Other stuff is actually now taken care of, but so many people request different things all the time. It's not a bad situation, just inconvenient at times.

"Mod Squad" is the Principal and the Assist

May 4, 2006

Getting a new phone today! Yay!

Allergies are bad this morning.

Years from now, people who discover this journal will think I had [Multiple Sclerosis because my handwriting is] so sloppy. But I was usually in a moving vehicle when writing.

May 6, 2006

Lazy day, sort of. I really deserve a lot of rest this weekend.

Why am I so emotional, though?

Shane has been creeping into my mind.

When I see him, I get a very specific schoolgirl crush feeling. I don't look at him, because if I look at him, he'll know. I am happier on the days we don't say much. Yet those are tough days, too.

His broad shoulders, deep voice, strong forearms, long legs…those things comfort me even though they don't "belong" to me. On Thursday, all I wanted to do was bury myself in his chest, and hold him, and be held.

May 10, 2006—Just before midnight

The past 48 hours have been crazy, like I'm in the middle of one big sob.

Yesterday afternoon, Shane resigned. Suddenly…we found out via email from [our supervisor]. The reasons why are his story to tell, not mine. My day yesterday was ruined, as was that of Monique, my AmeriCorps member. Shane is so loved.

I emailed him a few sentences. I told him that I didn't have to say how much I would miss him, or how much I owe to him. That as his friend, of course I wanted to know why, but that I'd find out when it was my time.

That I remembered every single conversation and correspondence that we'd had.

I don't remember what else I said. I do remember that the moment he'd read it, I had just had a heated discussion with the parent of an expelled student.

This man comes to me and asks if I am okay. I say yes, and then I discuss the parent, but I know he really meant "Are we okay?"

After I finish my story and the other Site Directors have laughed and told me that it will be okay, Shane took me outside to talk. I asked him "Why are you leaving?" and he told me.

After he explained everything, I told him that I believed he was doing the right thing. I hugged him…Jesus Christ, that was the best hug of my life. He is just the right size. His arms wrapped perfectly around me; my head fit right under his chin and neck…

We headed back toward the office and I found the guts to tell him…that the best part of coming to work was also the worst part. That I got to see him every day, but I had to see him every day. That I am attracted to someone that I can't have. And that I had very often retreated from him—distanced myself to make things less complicated.

To my surprise, he admitted the same. I didn't expect him to say that he was attracted to me, mostly because every day I feel fat and undesirable.

I think I felt vindicated somehow. Sure, he reiterated the fact that he had a boyfriend—that he lives with—but not as a way to deflect me. I think he said "I'm not supposed to be attracted to you, but I am."

So…that's what it is. I have no intention of going further. Shane has a man, and I am cool with that. I think I just needed to get the feelings off my chest. And I got the bonus of knowing that he felt similarly, yet we're both mature enough to know the boundaries.

But two things made it feel so good…his embrace…and this:

When I hugged him the first time, I felt my afro in his face, so I apologized. He told me not to, and that he liked my 'fro. Then he put his fingers in my hair and rubbed my scalp.

He did it again after our "revelations" as we went back in the office. It is probably the most intimate I will ever be with him.

I need to find the man who can make me feel like Shane does: safe, secure, attractive, loved.

…when I feel like this again, I know I will have found the one.

WRITE AS THOUGH NO ONE IS READING

January 3, 2009

I think my new year's resolution will be to write as though no one is reading. My writing has become very aware of itself over the years due to being such an avid blogger, as well as things like Facebook encouraging you to tell people what you're doing in short sound bites.

And then the comments. The endless comments. Especially when you've written something particularly well. Positive feedback is a great thing, but at the same time, it's kind of weird writing something and knowing someone will comment, because then you inevitably write to them, and then *for* them, rather than for yourself.

Maybe this happens with all writers. I don't know. I know at one point I used to be in love with E. Lynn Harris' writing until I grew to hate it. I felt like he stopped writing for me and started writing for heterosexual women.

When I first wrote *Lazarus*, people used to ask me if I wanted to be the next E. Lynn Harris. Instead of being humble and saying, "I really respect the work of E. Lynn, but I hope to become the first and best 'Rashid Darden' I can be," I would say "Who is E. Lynn Harris?" smile, laugh, and talk some more about *Lazarus*.

Yeah, I'm a dick. My prophyte Sadat was probably the first person to call me that and I took it as a compliment. It's not that writers have to be ruthless. But you've definitely got to have a personality. Being on the road in 2005 and 2006 showed me that some people are really ready for the writer's life and others aren't. I don't think I was one hundred percent ready, but I definitely had the chops. Right now, I'm still not totally ready to immerse myself in writing again. It's extraordinarily challenging to be a writer with real responsibilities.

I really fucked up some things in my life for a few years there when it came to personal responsibility, debt, obligations, etc. Writing doesn't pay the rent for me. It could, sure. Maybe I just don't want it bad enough yet. But I also know that I have a lot of talents in addition to writing which will pay the bills. Writing, for me, was always just plain fun. And once I'm just a little more stable in my career, then I can get back to the fun aspects of writing fiction which I miss so much.

I INTEND FOR 2009 TO BE DIFFERENT FOR ME

January 9, 2009

I intend for 2009 to be different for me.

I have no intentions on dating anyone. That is, I'm not going to go seeking a man, a boyfriend, a husband, whatever it is that I typically have this longing for. I plan to be devoted to my work. Work is Damien Ministries, Alpha Phi Alpha, and Alpha Phi Omega. I've been blessed with expanded responsibilities in all of those realms, and I am ready for them. I'm young, single, no kids – this is the time to "make it happen" so to speak, and "take what's mine." I suppose I sound like Puff Daddy.

Of course I know in my heart that I'm lonely. I helped a kid tie a necktie today at Noyes before the memorial service for those students who died in the fire.

I helped a kid tie a tie. Just like my grandfather did for me.

I looked at him and thought "I want one." My coworker later asked me which one of the kids was mine when he saw three fair-skinned children with curly hair walk by.

I turn 30 this year. I absolutely do not want a child right this second. I want to be devoted to Damien Ministries, Alpha Phi Alpha, and Alpha Phi Omega, not because I am escaping anything or not dealing with my problems, but because now is the time. I am young. I have energy. I am healthy. I have ideas and enthusiasm.

On another level, I also want to be an example that one can be active in both a social fraternity and a service fraternity at the same time; that one is not a steppingstone to the other but can complement each other nicely if your heart is into it.

But when it comes to dating…no, now isn't the time. It's hard for me to put into words why it isn't the time, but I'll try.

I used to believe that "it" wouldn't happen for me. People swore to me that it would happen when I wasn't looking. And, I don't know, I never *truly* thought I was looking. So when I would find a guy I liked, I think I would be convinced he might be the one I wasn't looking for. And when it didn't work out, I'd feel crappy all over again because I knew two things. First, oh my gosh, what the fuck, did I really just get hurt all over again? Second, maybe I was "looking" after all.

So maybe, just maybe, I have to do a little bit more than just saying "I'm not looking" – maybe I have some more lessons to learn about myself that have absolutely nothing to do with dating.

I know that one of those lessons will be to learn how to deal with my addiction to food and how to verbalize to my physician that my weight loss has to be related to my mental health. (Although I didn't intend to discuss this in depth, it really discouraged me when I told my doctor about my attempts at changing my diet and he just dismissed them without truly doing a full history of the situation. I am going to explain this to him on my next visit.)

I know another lesson will be how to translate successes I've had in certain areas into others. Being an Alpha teaches me how to be charismatic in Alpha Phi Omega; being in APO teaches me how to be more patient in Alpha. Damien Ministries gives me the compassion I need to work with others; Heads Up taught me lessons I recently mentioned in a status message on Facebook: friends can be enemies and sometimes even your enemies have your best interests at heart.

All of those lessons can, in both abstract and concrete ways, can be applied to relationships, just as much as the values that they teach: manly deeds, love for all mankind, being a leader, being a friend, serving the poorest of the poor, teaching – learning – leading.

Everything I do is preparing me to be a better lover, a better friend, a better husband, a better father. I don't have to date while I'm learning these things.

Another way to put this is that I am okay with being selfish for right now.

However, how easy it is to backslide.

If there's a phrase meaning "more pitiful than a hopeless romantic" then please let me know, because I have a wonderful headshot to send Miriam-Webster if they need an example of one. I'm one of those people who does believe that it can happen to me from the most unlikely of people and situations.

It's easy for me to romanticize even the most trivial of things…just today I found out a dude I would have loved to have gotten to know in another context has a MOTHERfuckin boyfriend. (Say it aloud with "mother" an octave higher. Thanks.) Keep in mind me and this dude have never once even spoken on that level, but it was my fault for letting my mind wander in that direction in the first place. Mentally and emotionally, I don't do things in the proper order. I jump from "Hey, he's a nice guy" to "I have to have him" without the simple diligence of figuring out if he's even taken.

After just having typed that entire paragraph, I realize that this actually happened to me twice this week about two different dudes. Do you see now why I don't need to date? Not because they're all taken (which is funny, by the way) but because in just one week, I didn't internalize well enough a lesson the first time around.

I have so much to learn.

I am not giving up on dating, I just don't want to date right now until I get myself together. If it happens, it happens, but I'm not looking for it to happen. I wish it would happen, but I will not create or manipulate situations for them to happen. I have my priorities for at least the next year and I am cool with them.

My friends and acquaintances know that I'm an amateur historian, particularly that of any aspect of the collegiate fraternal movement. My friend bought me a biography of Nellie Quander, the most revered incorporator of Alpha Kappa Alpha Sorority. The book was awesome and was written by her nephew. AKAs know her significance as an incorporator and the book goes into more than enough detail about that aspect of the sorority's history.

I was far more fascinated by Nellie Quander's life prior to and beyond the storied events of 1913. She was the kind of woman I admire…didn't generally take any shit from anyone and threw herself into her work and her organizations (and boy was she active in lots of them, including church). She had a lot of qualities I liked, especially her reputation as a stern, but fair educator and leader.

But what struck me about her was actually her similarities to me in activities and in demeanor, so much so that I jokingly began calling myself Nelroy Quander.

She had a legendary beef with her blood sister that led to a 40-year brooding silence between them. This is not a horn-tooting moment, but I am pretty sure that I could hold a grudge for 40 years if I wanted to.

She was very offended at lapses in proper protocol. In fact, she seemed very offended by lots of things. I'm pretty sensitive to things which could be perceived as personal slights. Why just today I went off on an old church lady in a staff meeting because I was tired of her talking to me any kind of way – and it seemed like she didn't take me seriously because I was young. I could have let it go, but I didn't.

The saddest part about the story of Nellie Quander is that she died alone, and her body wasn't discovered for two days. She never married, was not close to her extended family, and was probably closer to sorority members than blood relatives. Was she lonely, even though surrounded by so many people who considered her a good leader and savior of a whole sorority?

I mean, Nellie Quander gets mad respect.

But she died alone and went undiscovered for two days. No spouse, no children, no legacy.

Though I wish to have Quander-esque accolades bestowed upon me in life, I would trade them in for the chance at familial tranquility. A husband. Children. A legacy.

Nellie was 30 when she pledged AKA. I was 20 when I pledged APO and 23 when I became an Alpha. Maybe my ten-year jump on the fraternal bandwagon will prevent me from the same fate as the much-respected woman. Maybe I am doing just enough right where my heart won't be closed to the possibility of happiness.

Maybe I will find a way to live and let live, to forgive the ever-growing list of people who I have felt wronged me in some way.

Maybe I will be able to realize when the right guy has finally come along – when I wasn't looking.

I don't think I am doomed to the same fate. But I know that the decision I am currently making to focus on anything but a relationship could easily take me down that path.

I'm not worried. I know I will make the right decisions. I know my friends will intervene if I make the wrong ones. I expect them to. I will never put my own happiness behind Damien Ministries, Alpha, and APO. It's just that right now, those things do give me happiness and I'm going to run with it for a little while longer.

there's a certain point when you have to stop apologizing and just step aside so somebody else can do the job.

-- June 18, 2010

MY INDEPENDENCE DAY

JULY 4, 2010

Just after midnight, I completed my third novel, *Epiphany*, and sent it to a friend to be edited. Or proofread. One of those. Then I went to sleep.

All day, I complained that I didn't know of any cookouts going on save one in Howard County, which is literally The Boondocks. But it was fine, because I was finishing a staycation of sorts. I hadn't been at work since my birthday, June 25. As far as I was concerned, to not have anything to do was a blessing. I didn't have any particular obligations and I was still feeling like king of the world for finishing *Epiphany*.

For the sake of irreverence, I pretended to be sad that America didn't belong to the British anymore, leaving voicemails in fun British accents to a few of my friends, and changing my Facebook profile picture to the Crown Jewels, and later, a young Queen Elizabeth. I did it to be funny, but I also did it to preemptively block out all of the victimization and pity-porn updates about how black people aren't free, so why are we celebrating? Or more accurately, we weren't free in 1776, so why should we acknowledge this day?

(I literally just sighed.)

It goes without saying that I am an American. I never felt more American than I did on four different occasions:

The first: when I studied in Moscow for a month when I was in high school. Not only did I have to learn to speak a different language, but I had to understand a new alphabet. Russia was one of the greatest experiences of my youth, but it's not for the weak-hearted. You will feel every bit of American if you go, particularly if you are African American.

The second: when I went to England when I was in college. Granted, there was much less of a culture shock than any in Russia, but you still had to be aware of your surroundings and realize that people really will hate you just because you're American.

The third: 9/11. Enough said.

And tonight: the Fourth.

Just after 9pm, I noticed the familiar pops and whistles of neighborhood fireworks. I really don't know when this began (I do not remember it when I lived at 2nd and Kennedy as a child), but somehow fireworks began to be launched from places like ball fields, traffic triangles, and school playgrounds. When I lived in Riggs Park, I could just walk down to LaSalle and see them. I just moved here, back to Kennedy Street, this year, so I wasn't sure what I would see.

When I heard the action beginning, I leaned out of my kitchen window and saw nothing but fireworks from the eastern horizon all the way to the west, over Rock Creek Park. I wasn't sure how far I was able to see, but I imagined that I must be seeing the annual Riggs Park fireworks show in the east. At some point, I saw fireworks appear to be launching from the middle of Kennedy Street itself, shooting upward into the sky. Looking northwest there were more fireworks, probably from that park where Missouri Avenue forms the outer boundary of Brightwood Park. These barely reached over the tree line, but they never seemed to stop. Immediately before my window, behind the empty lot where the old stench emanated late this past winter, there were black boys lighting firecrackers. Behind them, beyond the apartment building were intermittent fireworks. There were the best ones, exploding in white cauliflower-like bursts. On Kennedy Street, in front of Odalis, a group of Latino youth lit fireworks that I remembered from my own youth – the ones that make fire hydrant-high light shows, along with several other kinds which stretched past the height of the buildings. Finally, somewhere in the west, several different shows competed with purple and blue explosions.

Sulfuric smells quickly permeated the air, but it didn't bother me. The soundtrack of this scene wasn't a cacophony, but a calming, reassuring series of taps and booms which were reminiscent of a hailstorm.

How could I not feel American? How could I not feel free?

I am 31 years old and keenly aware of the gifts that God has given me, which only begin with being born in absolutely the right country at undoubtedly the right time. Yes, my ancestors were slaves. They would have wanted me to know my history, but not let my history contribute to a collective anger and disenfranchisement that prevents me from moving forward.

My ancestors tell me that I was never a slave and wasn't born to be one. They fought so that I could live – how dare I mire myself in a fight that I can't even begin to understand?

I say it again – I was not a slave. I do not have the right to downplay or belittle any celebration of our Independence Day.

Our independence day.

My skin may not be the same color of George Washington or Thomas Jefferson, but our values are both shared and colorless. How can I not feel a kinship to them? Our paths were different, our origins night and day. But just as my ancestors who were in shackles made sacrifices so that I would be free, so did these men, whether their intention was for my freedom or not.

On Father's Day, it was stated that all fathers should receive their due whether they were in their children's lives or not. What makes Independence Day so different?

When I look out onto Kennedy Street and see Latino owned businesses alongside black owned businesses… when I see first- and second-generation Latino youth engaging in the cultural traditions of my own youth… when I see the fireworks, hear the booms, smell the sulfur… I know that I am home. I know that I am free.

I am free to sit in my apartment and pine away for a man that I know I love, embracing the hopeless romantic in me that I tried to hide. If I want to spend two, three, four hours just thinking about him and being giddy and plotting my next move – I can do that. And because this is DC, I can fantasize about marrying this man and having my government acknowledge it. And because this is America, I know that I can fight toward federal recognition of a marriage between two men.

I am free also to support my Latino and Ethiopian and other immigrants who live next to me, stand next to me at bus stops, share their language, culture, food, and traditions with me – I can do that, too. I acknowledge that I stand on another culture's land and benefit from so many atrocities which happened to their ancestors. I acknowledge this, but I do not move. I do not leave. This is my home. Their culture is my culture. I do not get angry because immigrants came and "took over" my neighborhood. I am glad that I am challenged and stretched and get to see my neighborhood evolve. As well it should.

Life is so fleeting. I feel American today because I know it is fleeting, yet my culture and my traditions live on in a new generation. A year from now, my street will not be the same. Tomorrow, my street will not be the same. I am not the same person that I was when I began writing.

Today is my independence day. I free myself from the perception of victimization at the hands of an unknown machine. I free myself from forces which are used to distract me from my independence. The forces are not negative – *I* transform them into distractions and am further taken from my goals. Who am I to put my faith, my time, my effort into man-made constructs rather than using my gifts and talents to add to the canon of literature?

This is what I was born to do. I was not born a brother of Alpha Phi Omega. I was not born a brother of Alpha Phi Alpha. I was not born to be on Facebook. I was not born to be on Twitter.

I was born to lean outside of my window, watch the fireworks, smell the smoke, and listen to the heartbeat of the city. I was born to hear the echoes of my own past and see shadows of myself holding sparklers in my back yard, jumping on mini-trampolines, and eating watermelon and not being ashamed of it.

I am a Washingtonian. I am an American. I am not ashamed of my country, our past, and our mistakes. Nor am I ashamed of our successes. I was born to be here. I was born to be *now*.

I was born to be born, to live, and to die. I was born to love. I *am* love. I love. I am free.

Cooperation is overrated. Doing as I say is a guaranteed win.

--May 8, 2012

PICTURE IT

Halloween Day 2012, Downtown Washington, DC.

I shared this message when my IndieGoGo Campaign for Birth of a Dark Nation *went live.*

That was the last day that I worked a "regular" full-time job. For four months, I had endured the emotional and physical stress of working at a nonprofit organization which didn't deserve my talents. I'm sorry for the bluntness, not sorry for the truth: that I had been duped into working for an organization that promised me freedom, creativity, and leadership.

My first intern came and went during my first month; during the second, my grandmother had died, and I had asked my roommate to leave our living situation. I had never experienced stress like that which I was enduring personally, but I was dealing with a callousness from my leadership that didn't seem to care. I'd lost a major source of income (my roommate) and the rock of my family. But they didn't care a single day after the funeral passed. Later, I'd become ill for a week and the executive director literally emailed me every day, asking and expecting to do work.

I'm sick. I'm tired. Why won't she let me recover?

I had had it with the micromanaging, of the sketchiness, of literally the smell of the leadership distracting me from working.

I decided to leave. The crazy lady I worked for texted me a dozen times, called me eight times, and threatened to withhold my final check.

I felt like Sarah in *Labyrinth*: "You have no power over me."

[I am sure that there is a Bible verse which is more accurate than that, but I'm sorry that I know *Labyrinth* better than I know the Bible.]

They had no power over me. I realized I could no longer give energy to projects I didn't believe in. I could not write grant proposals for foundations that I knew could spend their money better elsewhere. I could not continue to ignore the fact that I came to work feeling ill every day.

They had no power over me. No more words would be wasted on emails. No more words would be wasted on applications. No more words would be wasted on narratives.

They had no power over me. The micromanaging would end. The unsanitary conditions would end. The jealousy would end. The lies would end.

I provided my notice and left to do what I was born to do: Write novels.

There may be a day that I return to an office setting. I hope not, because I enjoy the struggle of writing. It is my own struggle and I answer to me.

But today, I write. Yesterday, I wrote. Tomorrow, I will write some more.

This is what the #BlackVampireProject means to me. I'm doing it so our stories may be told in every genre. I'm doing it for all of the writers who can't just get up and go, like I did. I risked a lot. I gave up a whole hell of a lot. But I did it to be myself.

That is why in every biography you will read of me, I insist that the phrase "Rashid Darden is a novelist" is the first thing you read. I am not a nonprofit professional first. I am not black, gay, or male first.

Rashid Darden is a novelist.

For all that I walked away from, for all that I have sacrificed, I hope you will consider funding the #BlackVampireProject so that my novel "Birth of a Dark Nation" will get the proper start with professional editing, professional cover design, and professional publicity and public relations. I also hope that you will invest in this project so that I may inspire a new generation of authors through a creative writing tour during National Novel Writing Month 2013.

Thanks for reading.... thanks for listening... thanks for giving.

--Rashid

If somebody puts a call out into the universe,
who am I to say that I'm not the response?
---May 21, 2012

I think people on Pinterest be lying

--June 24, 2012

I went out three nights in a row. Jesus must be coming back.

--June 26, 2013

You sure got a lot of questions for somebody who been doing websites since Moses walked the earth.

--June 30, 2014

BITTERSWEET
JUNE 30, 2014

The end of June is always bittersweet for me... I have tried hard not to commit my friend Maya's date of passing to memory, so I end up personally commemorating it on the last day of the month. I don't really want to remember that my friend died three days after my birthday.

But whenever I make a big decision in my life - especially around this time of year - I know it is Maya who is looking over my shoulder, whispering "Yes... put yourself first. Walk away from the things that aren't working for you. The time to fight has passed; it's now time to stand up for yourself."

Yes, Maya was sweet, but she was also a humdinger just like me! So when I have those moments where I'm like "Mannnnnnn forget this" I know that Maya would have been on the other end of my phone line telling me "Yeah…forget that."

I love you, Maya, and I miss you. You taught me well. I hope you're enjoying my friends Jimi and Donald and Derek and Terrance and TreNai and Chris and Jabriel.

NEGOTIATIONS: A *DARK NATION* STORY

2015

"Look, bitch. The first thing you're going to do is release our brother. Then maybe--if you're lucky--we can discuss working together. But until then, you're shit out of luck if you think the Razadi are going to negotiate with genie terrorists!"

My brown finger punctuated each syllable of my tirade. Dante and I stood feet away from the two olive-skinned Amazons in a dark, underground parking garage in downtown Philadelphia. The stagnant air was thick with the scent of gasoline and lingering exhaust fumes.

"Justin, don't!" Dante put his hand on my shoulder and tried to pull me back toward our white work van, away from the silver Acura belonging to the women.

"Don't stifle your *ipsaji*," the beautiful Djinn purred.

"Listen. We don't want any trouble. We just want John back." Dante reasoned with the women as I seethed.

"John Irons?" the second Djinn said. "Is he named after your Uncle John?"

"You mind your business," I spat.

The Djinn women shimmered into a pillar of flames and then disappeared.

"Oh God," Dante whimpered.

In seconds, I was surrounded on two sides by heatless fire, crackling and popping inches from my face.

"Perhaps we got off on the wrong foot," a disembodied woman's voice menaced.

"I am not afraid of you," I said firmly, though my heart raced. The fire phased back into the women's forms. They were tall and stately. The one to my left wore a long, dark gray mink coat. Her curly hair fell over the collar. A short black dress hugged her body, accentuating her hips and breasts. The one to my right wore a black maxi dress and a mid-length black leather coat. Her straight hair was tied in a ponytail at the base of her neck.

"We don't want you to be afraid of us. Look at me," the one on the left said.

I resisted her request.

"Justin, look at me," she repeated. I slowly turned my gaze toward her. She was tall, broad, and built. Her shapely legs supported a substantial upper half, with round breasts threatening to peek through her low-cut dress.

"My eyes are up here," she added. I sharply looked up to see her round face smiling at me, with just one dimple on the right. It was nearly impossible to tell what race she was. She could just as easily have passed for Ethiopian as she could have Arab or Italian, much like her sister in arms.

"See, that wasn't so hard, was it? Listen, sweetie. My name is Khadijah. This is Destiny. Now that you know our names, you don't have to refer to us as that dreadful slur. I mean really, 'genie?' That word died decades ago."

"And if you use the g-word again, we'll slice you open from the inside out," Destiny said.

I looked at her sideways.

"Give us John Irons," I said.

"We will," Khadijah said. "But you have something we want."

She moved close to me and touched her warm hand to my chest. It slid down my torso to my belt, which she grabbed and pulled me close to her. Destiny rubbed my body from behind.

"Are you kidding me right now?" I asked, pulling away from both of them and stumbling to Dante's side.

"Ladies," he said. "You can't be serious."

"As a heart attack," Khadijah cooed.

"Listen, those are just old wives' tales," he continued. "Djinn and Razadi…it just doesn't…it doesn't *work*."

"What are you talking about?" I whispered.

"He doesn't know!" Destiny said with surprise. She laughed and stood closely to Khadijah, loosely locking arms with her.

"We've always been good to your people," Khadijah began. "When you spread out over the continent, Djinn kept you safe. We served you as best we could. Those of us who walk the earth, at least. We know. We know how important Razadi are. We know all about the New Dawn."

Dante and I looked at each other in astonishment.

"Now we're speaking your language, aren't we?" Khadijah asked rhetorically. "It's a cold, cruel world out there, Justin, teeming with vampires and…well…white people. Imagine a world run by Djinn and Razadi. We *are* children of the sun, after all. So let's make some more, okay?"

"What? You can't be for real," I said.

"Khadijah…Destiny…Razadi and Djinn can't reproduce. That is just legend. Mythology. You need to know that Razadi men are infertile. We can't make babies. We can barely make other Razadi!"

"That's not what we heard," Destiny said.

"Well you heard wrong," Dante said.

"That's what John tried to tell us," Khadijah said. "Put yourself in our shoes. We never meet Razadi. Ever. Y'all just don't see fit to live in Philadelphia. And that's cool. But for us to see John Irons…all six feet six inches of him, walking down Germantown Avenue looking all good, smelling fragrant like all you Razadi do. How could we resist?"

"It's people out here dying in a war between daywalkers and nightwalkers and you tried to rape John?" I asked incredulously.

"Well…we were nice about it!" Destiny said.

"John is a great guy, really he is," Khadijah continued. "But…even after making nice, hanging out with him showing him proper Djinn hospitality…he just wouldn't give up the goods. So we…"

"What?" Dante asked.

"We kinda locked him up in an iron casket for a few months."

I bared my fangs and hissed at the wenches.

"Now don't get all hissy," Khadijah said. "We knew somebody would come looking eventually."

"Eventually?" I lisped through my fangs.

"All we want…is one night. You for me…and Dante for Destiny. Or vice versa. Your choice."

"No. It's not going to happen. We can get you anything else, but-"

"Wait." I held my hand up, interrupting Dante. "You mean to tell me all you want is to get fucked by a Razadi and you will give us John?"

"That's the long and short of it," Khadijah said.

"Hopefully long," Destiny quipped. I raised my eyebrow.

"Um, excuse me," Dante said. "Sidebar please?"

Dante grabbed me by the arm and walked me about ten feet away from the Djinn women. In the fluorescent glimmer of one of the few lights in the garage, Dante appeared fearful.

"You can't be serious! We can't fuck these broads!" he said.

"Why not? Does vagina repulse you that much?"

"No! I fucked plenty bitches in my day!" He puffed and said it with his chest.

"So what makes this different? Yo, they have John Irons. And all they want is this dick."

Dante looked toward the ground, avoiding my gaze.

"We can't catch no disease. Not like Djinn have diseases, though. And we can't get 'em pregnant, but they don't seem to want to admit that to themselves. And if we do it, we get J.I. I don't see how we could lose."

"I mean…have you ever even done it with a woman before?"

"How hard could it be?" I grinned through my fangs.

"You wild," Dante said.

"Hey. When this is over…I'm all yours. However you want me." I leaned into Dante and kissed him on the lips.

"Okay," he whispered.

"Ladies!" I called stomping back toward them as they waited for us.

"Yes?" Khadijah responded.

"First things first. Where is John Irons?"

"One floor above us in an iron box in the bottom of an empty dumpster. He's safe. Hibernating, but alive."

"Good. Now, as for us? We'll do you. But this ain't no overnight shit. If you want to get fucked by a Razadi, you get fucked right here, right now. No candles and incense, no Luther Vandross playlist."

Khadijah and Destiny looked at each other and shrugged ever so slightly.

"We can live with that," Khadijah said.

"And no round two," Dante added. "Once we come, that's it. And don't call us no more."

The women smiled.

"Oh, one time is all we need," Khadijah said.

"And all we can stand," Dante added.

"We'll even let you drink," Destiny said.

"Word?" I asked.

"Mmm-hmm. But you know Djinn blood is…potent."

I sized up the women one last time, deciding which one I would try on for size. They both were beautiful, in spite of their manipulations and coercion. They were anything any regular Philadelphia dudes would want: legs, titties, ass, and long hair.

But we weren't from Philadelphia and we weren't regular dudes. We were Razadi, daywalking vampires with roots in West Africa. Tricked into slavery by a rival tribe. Subdued by nightwalking Italian mercenaries. Stolen from Africa and spread like dandelion seeds across the Western Hemisphere during the darkest days in the history of the diaspora. We were hunted by nightwalkers for our ability to walk in the sun. And now we were lusted after by Djinn for our seed.

It was hard out here for a vamp.

"So what are you waiting for?" Khadijah asked. She slid her panties down her legs and kicked them to the side.

I looked at Dante, who was already salivating at the prospect of Djinn blood, if not Djinn pussy.

"Let's go!" I said.

Destiny and Khadijah's eyes glowed orange as we stormed toward them. Dante unbuckled his belt. The red band of his boxer briefs emerged as his black pants slid down on his hips. I looked at his face, fangs bared, dreadlocks crowning his head like snakes, and eyes wild. He looked at me and smiled.

I glanced downward and began removing my shirt. Dante reached over and patted my now-flat stomach. It was a sight I had a hard time getting used to after years of obesity. The Razadi diet of blood and vegetables had transformed me.

I tingled from my stomach to my fingertips and toes, and back to my manhood. The Djinn women giggled as we approached them.

"Kiss him," Destiny instructed Dante as she took off her leather jacket. Dante grabbed me by the neck with one hand and forced his mouth on mine. His tongue tasted every inch of mine until I could hardly breathe.

Khadijah rubbed her hand on the front of my pants, feeling my growing erection.

"We're all friends here," she said in my ear as Dante continued kissing me. I backed off from him, grinned, and refocused on Khadijah.

"Are-" I began, but her mouth was on mine in an instant. Her mink hit the ground. Destiny slid Dante's pants down and my eyes fluttered shut.

Khadijah's mouth was hot, hotter than Dante's, and she tasted sweet, something like a mango to the tenth power. I was intoxicated by her essence and intrigued by her body. My hands grabbed her hips and my mouth made a trail from her neck to her breasts. I found a nipple and began to suck. She moaned softly.

Dante hoisted Destiny onto the hood of her Acura and dove into her repeatedly. She yelped each time he smashed into her. He looked over his shoulder at me and winked.

We were so turned on.

The fingers of my right hand walked their way from Khadijah's thigh to her vulva, already slick with her juices.

"Fuck me, daywalker."

We slowly ascended a few feet into the air as she threw one foot, then another over my shoulders. The atmosphere turned from the sickly darkness of the garage into a bright orange of life and Djinn fire. I entered her and felt a calm wash over me. My dick plunged into her, over and over, matching the rhythm of my *ipsaji*, who fucked just feet away from me.

I blinked. We were weightless in an endless vista of flames, feeling only the heat between our bodies. Khadijah's breasts bounced with each thrust. Unbound by gravity, she now rode me, as Destiny reversed her position into a split on top of Dante. We groaned, grunted, and screamed silently as the crackles of the flames muted our passions.

As we climaxed simultaneously, Dante and I sank our fangs into the Djinn, and pierced their necks. Our mouths were flooded with a blood that was at once sweet and spicy. I drank this intoxicating brew and felt transformed and transported, into something I'd never been before, yet always was; to someplace I'd never been, yet felt like home.

As quickly as the moment came, it went. The orange flames died down and flickered out. We were in the garage, in the darkness, leaning against the side of our white van with our pants around our ankles.

"Thanks for the gift," Destiny said as she kissed an exhausted and sweaty Dante on the cheek.

"Your brother is on the next level up. I'm sorry I couldn't have him, but I am ever so grateful for the chance to have you," Khadijah whispered in my ear. I couldn't move. I watched the women put their clothes back on and casually get into their car, as though the best orgasm of my life hadn't just happened.

"Boys," Destiny said as she put the key in the ignition. "Wake up and get your man."

I snapped out of the stupor and looked down at myself. Sticky ejaculate slowly dripped from my penis and onto the floor. Dante blinked several times and became present as well.

"Shit," he said.

"Let's go."

We pulled up our pants and put on our shirts as we ran to the upper level of the garage, seeking the dumpster where our brother would be.

"I smell him. It's faint, but he's here," Dante said.

"There's the dumpster!" I announced. We sprinted to the royal blue box and hopped over the side, landing squarely on the inside with the precision of gold medal gymnasts.

The iron coffin was exactly where the women said it would be.

"Thank goodness," I exhaled. "Let's find a crowbar or something."

As I looked around the dumpster, Dante already easily broke the chains with his bare hands.

"Damn," I said.

"Temporary Djinn infusion," he said. "Drinking humans is like getting drunk. Drinking Djinn is like cocaine."

I nodded vigorously. Together we pried open the iron box.

John's immense body laid stiff as a board but didn't look dead. There was still color in his face. His mouth was turned downward into a scowl.

"John," Dante said sternly. "Wake up. You're safe."

John didn't move.

"John, my name is Justin," I began, lightly shaking his shoulder. "Justin Kena. We just rescued you from-"

John's eyes opened and he hissed, fangs totally elongated. His huge arm reached out and he grabbed me by the throat. I immediately tried to take his hand from my neck, but he was too strong for me. I struggled to breathe.

"John, no! He's one of us!" Dante shouted as he tried to pry John's fingers from my throat.

"I don't know this man," John growled.

"A lot happened when you were away! Trust me, he is one of us!"

John effortlessly pulled me toward him inside the box. He sniffed my face, even as I struggled to breathe.

"It's true," I whispered. "I was turned."

We locked eyes. John was angry, scared, and sad all at once.

"Drink me," I gasped. "You must be so hungry. Do it."

John didn't need convincing. He loosened his grasp on me and bit my neck. I closed my eyes. The blood draining away from me felt heavenly, but I knew this wasn't a pleasure meal. I needed to earn John's trust after his months of captivity.

As he drank deeply, my hands found his face. I caressed him and concentrated.

I am one of you. I transmitted to his consciousness.

I sent him all of the memories that I had made with Dante, Victor, and the rest of the Razadi. The first day I'd met Dante on the stoop of the Masonic hall. The day Dante revealed himself to me. Our long walks across Washington. The day I was attacked by the nightwalker. My slow transformation into a daywalker. The day I was initiated into the tribe. Our rescue of Orlando.

The opening and closing of his jaw slowed down as he drank in my memories. His hands loosened, then tightened around me again, transitioning from the grip of control to the embrace of a friend.

He stopped drinking and pushed me away. His dark eyes welled up with tears.

"Hello, brother," he said.

"Hi," I said softly, with a smile and a nod.

"Are you okay Justin?" Dante asked me.

"I'm good. Let's get the hell out of here."

We pulled up John from his box. His legs were shaky, but he was strong. We leapt out of the smelly dumpster and slowly walked back toward our van on the lower level. Khadijah and Destiny were long gone.

As we sped out of the city, fireworks darted the night sky over the Schuylkill River.

"Happy New Year," Dante said to me from the driver's seat.

"Same to you," I responded. "You okay back there, JI?"

"Yes," he said quietly.

"We would have come for you sooner, but we didn't know," Dante said.

"I always check in."

"But the last time you left-"

"I *always* check in."

"You're right. You do. I'm really sorry, John. I really am."

The awkward silence filled the van like noxious fumes.

"What's a new year to people like us, anyway?" Dante asked to no one in particular.

"Djinn…Razadi…nightwalkers…and whatever else might be out there," I mused.

The city lights soon gave way to the dense and dark Pennsylvania forest. In a different life, when I was just a human, I might have been afraid of the forest, even though I grew up in a huge house at the edge of the woods. I was a skittish kid, the baby of the family who was afraid of monsters--the ones in my head, the ones in the woods, and the ones disguised as adults who preyed on kids for sex.

That skittish kid grew up to be a depressed, complacent adult with no road map for life. That adult met the Razadi and finally became who he was meant to be.

I was no longer afraid of the forest and the things that go bump in the night. I was now the one to be afraid of. *I* go bump in the night.

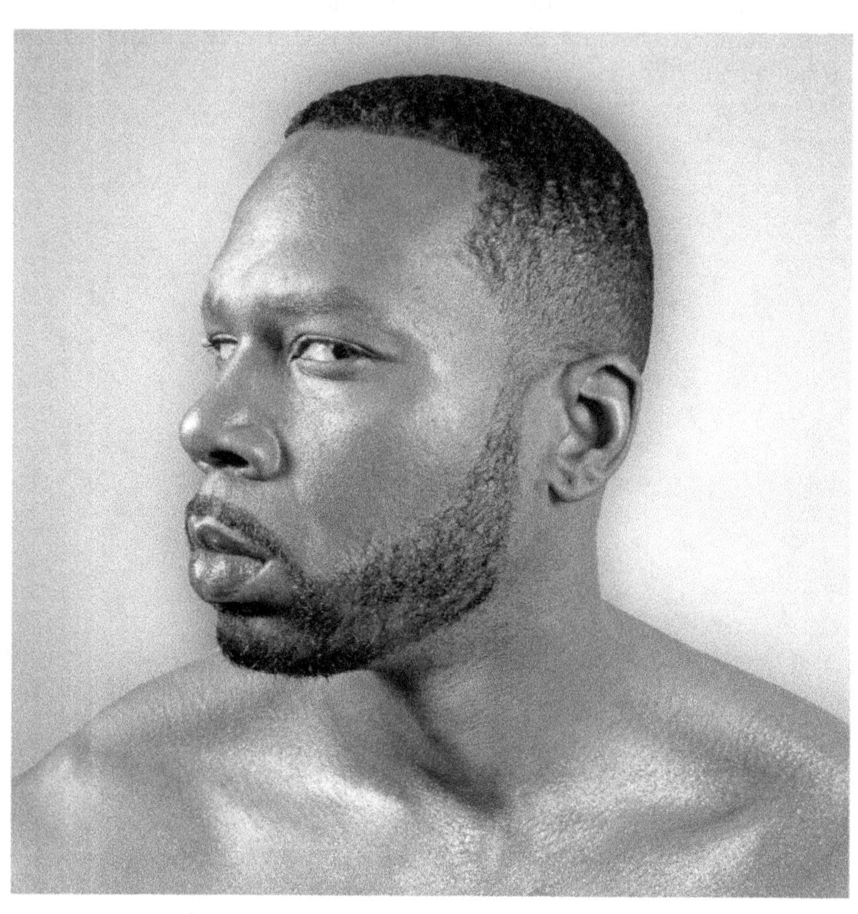

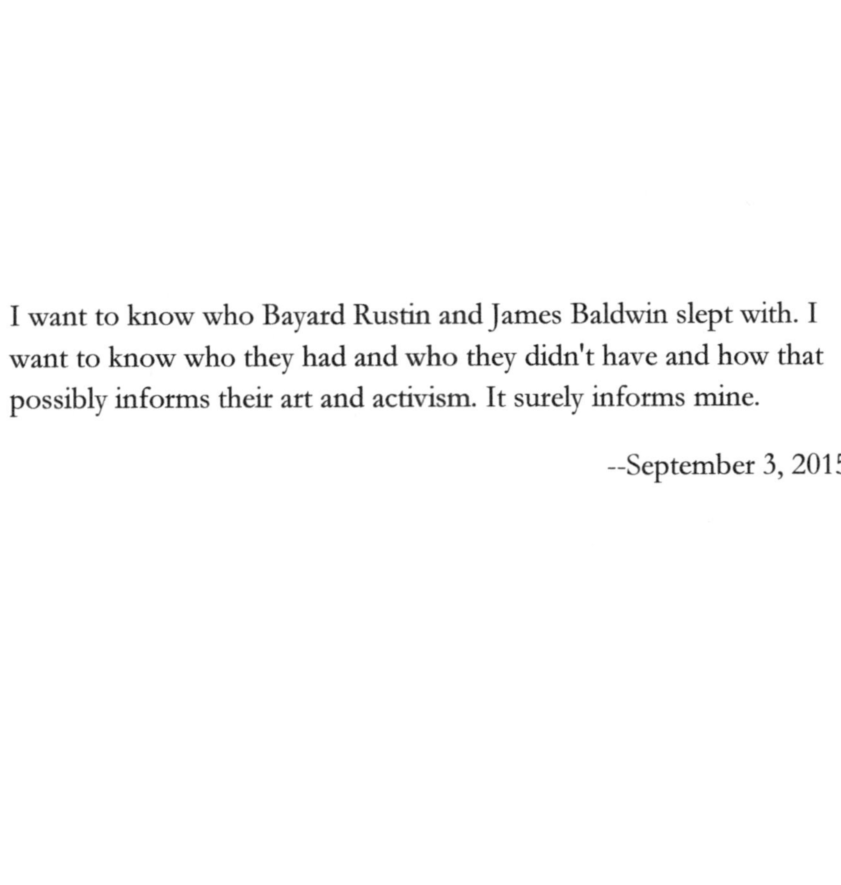

I want to know who Bayard Rustin and James Baldwin slept with. I want to know who they had and who they didn't have and how that possibly informs their art and activism. It surely informs mine.

--September 3, 2015

SMITH & JONES: YOUNG AMERICANS
2016

The mellow grooves of mid-90s R&B Christmas songs filled the dusty library while about forty people—mostly middle-aged black women—stuffed their faces with homemade cakes, cookies, and pies. This school had collectively decided long ago to forgo the experimentation of deviled eggs, tuna casseroles, or even tossed salad. No, these teachers said, "To hell with it" and decided every celebration would be an unofficial competition for the sweetest, sugariest, most diabetes-inducing gluten-rich delights. They'd take no more chances on Mr. Burton's potato salad, particularly after the year the entire science department went to the emergency room. Nor would further chances be given to old crossed-eyed Mrs. Sales, who most of us thought for certain washed her collard greens in her bathtub.

No matter the school system, be it public, private, or charter, there was one constant among all teachers: we loved to eat. It didn't matter what we were celebrating, or if we were celebrating at all. If someone said Christmas, Thanksgiving, Halloween, or just "long staff meeting" the call went out for the Old Lady Goon Squad to begin baking their delectable delights.

I didn't really want to go to this stupid holiday party, but I knew the Goon Squad would never let me live it down if I skipped it. Not only was the school Christmas party the biggest event of the year, it was also to be the final time I'd see Mr. Jones.

The school building's marble stairs were so old that there were curves in them, as though a giant had bounced down each one and left a butt print behind. In reality, it was just an eighty-year-old building that should have never used marble in a high school, not accounting for, you know, actual usage. But that was the 1940s in the nation's capital. Washington, DC at that time was a racially segregated city in which the many schools for white students looked like ornate palaces in comparison to the old, under-resourced buildings relegated to the black students.

Oh, how the times had changed. Coolidge High School was now a mostly black and Latino high school and had been so for many decades before my own 32 years of life. And now, in the post-Obama America and post-Marion Barry Washington, the white families were slowly coming back into the neighborhood. In another generation, Coolidge would probably be all white once more.

The Old Lady Goon Squad knew it and they held on to Coolidge for dear life. Now here's the thing: The Old Lady Goon Squad wasn't really all old ladies. In fact, only Edith Davis, the English Department Chair, was even near retirement age. They only seemed older than they were because they knew better than most about the "good old days" in public education, before the charter schools took root and began attracting the top students away from their neighborhood schools; the days before the mega-sized educational organizations with their strange corporate bedfellows began dropping unqualified and unprepared first-year teachers into the neediest schools.

It was hard out here for real teachers. Why did I ever choose this job?

My feet walked down the curved steps carefully as I prepared to leave the building.

"Mr. Smith!" A voice shrieked down from above. I looked up to see a bespectacled, round-faced, brown-skinned woman looking down on me over the railing.

"Hey Mrs. Washington," I said coolly. She peered at me over her glasses.

"I know you ain't leaving this building before the holiday party!" she said.

"No ma'am, I'm just going to my car to get my contribution!"

"Oh, you made something?" she asked.

"Nah, just bought one of those Walmart pies."

"Boy, you coulda kept that shit at home. Patti's pies ain't got nothing on *my* sweet potato pie! Believe that!"

"I believe it, ma'am," I smiled.

"Well hurry on back, we 'bout to start. And see if you can find Mr. Jones out there, will you?"

I exhaled.

"Yes ma'am…"

Pearl Washington, the Chemistry teacher, was like everybody's mama. If she said "hurry up" then she meant it and you'd damn well better hurry. She also cussed like a sailor when the students weren't around (and sometimes when they were), so I felt lucky she had only said "shit" once.

My gray coaches' jacket was nothing against the nippy December air and I thrust my hands as deep into the pockets as I could. Dumb move leaving my coat in the trunk of my car, but at least I knew it would be safe. These bad ass kids would steal anything that wasn't nailed down, even though I was one of their favorite teachers.

I came to Coolidge about five years ago to replace a retiring physical education teacher. I had just completed my Master of Arts in Teaching while substitute teaching around the city for a few years. Before that I had played some arena football and prayed for a chance to join the NFL. That opportunity never came, so my plan B was in full effect.

I popped open the trunk of my Mercedes Benz and quickly put on my leather jacket. I grabbed the two boxed pies and slammed the trunk shut.

"Damn, what did that trunk ever do to you?"

I immediately recognized the proper voice and pretended not to care as I looked over my shoulder.

"I just have a heavy hand, Mr. Jones," I said.

"Need some help?" he asked.

"Nah. The Goon Squad is looking for you, though."

"Word?"

I chuckled.

"Yeah. Word." I turned around fully and looked at him. From head to toe, he looked like the cool English teacher everyone wanted to take. His dreadlocks passed the shoulders of his buttoned black pea coat by about a foot. His lean legs were hidden by baggy denim. In fact, the only exposed skin on him was his oval face. a bright, sandy contrast against his jet-black eyebrows and beard. The frame of his glasses were also black—thin wire rims that he barely needed, but sat intentionally on his pointy nose, perhaps just a millimeter too long and a centimeter too wide, but perfect on him and for him.

"Why you laughing?" he asked.

"It kills me when you use slang. You ain't even from New York, saying 'word' like you straight outta Brooklyn."

"You always clown me for code switching. If black folks could just be okay with each other as they are, I wouldn't have to."

I looked sideways at him and began walking.

"You really think other black folks is why we code switch?"

"Black folks are why I code switch, yeah."

"You shoulda gone to Howard, my man. I don't know what they was teaching you at Hampshire."

"So had I gone to Howard, they woulda taught me how to hate whitey, too?"

"Here you go again. I don't hate white folks. All I'm saying is that code switching is what black folks have to do so we're not judged by white folks on our own culture, custom, style, and speech. White folks can be from the Midwest, New England, down South, or West Coast and not receive the level of discrimination black folks get for speaking in African American vernacular English."

"Tony."

"What?"

"I'm just fucking with you," he laughed. His teeth fit his face perfectly, long teeth and pointy canines matching his other long and slender features.

"Oh," I said.

"That's what they taught me at Hampshire. A fucking sense of humor."

"Ha ha, nigga. Let's hit this party."

We entered the school again, Mr. Jones with his boxes of cookies and me with my pies. The halls had been long cleared of students. As this was the last day of class before the Christmas holiday, every student who had even bothered to show up for school was eager to get home. The teachers, too, were eager to leave, but not before the dessert extravaganza.

"How long you staying?" I asked Mr. Jones.

"I guess until the end. I mean, it is my last day and all." He looked at me. I quickly looked down and watched my orange and gray New Balance tennis shoes touch the marble floor. We entered the long hallway toward the library in silence.

"Me and the old ladies are going to Takoma Station after this. You should come."

"I don't know."

"Don't be like this," he whispered.

"Don't leave," I hissed, still looking at the floor.

The youngest Old Lady Goon, Mrs. Nellie Warren, was the 38-year-old computer science teacher. She was tall, shapely and was proud of the white stripe down the center of her long, thick mane of hair.

"Took y'all long enough! It's time to eat!" she said unnaturally loudly for the hallway. She grabbed Mr. Jones' bag and my pies and let the door close behind her.

"Well that was rude," Mr. Jones said. I opened the door wide for him for him to pass through.

"Surprise!" the faculty and staff yelled in unison.

"Oh God," Mr. Jones said, covering his mouth with his hands. Over the dusty books and computers so old they seemed to be props from *Steve Jobs* hung a huge banner, painted by art students with extreme care in the school's colors of orange and gray: *Bon Voyage, Mr. Jones!* The staff continued clapping for our nearly departed friend while Mrs. Warren loudly, and off key began singing "For He's a Jolly Good Fellow." I joined in, only after being pinched on both sides by Mrs. Warren and Mrs. Washington, who had observed my utter lack of participation.

The principal reached out her hand and led Mr. Jones to the front of the room, just under the banner, while the rest of the faculty and staff finished up the song. Jones was smiling from ear to ear.

"Surprised you, huh?" she said. Mr. Jones nodded his head vigorously.

The principal was a young black woman in her forties or so. She did not come from the era when principals were old, wizened men and women who had waited their whole lives to be plucked from the obscurity of faculty. Instead, she came from the era when two years in a depressed school system, an online doctorate in education, and lip balm to alleviate years of ass-kissing were the pathway to a nearly six-figure job that was primarily about firing teachers and improving test scores.

Nobody liked her, but it wasn't her fault. Not really. She was just a principal.

"Mr. Jones, as you know this is our annual holiday party, but since we knew this was your last day here, we wanted to make it special. You've been with Coolidge for three and a half years and every single day has been special. You hit the ground running, not only bringing our kids on the bottom up, but raising the ceiling for our honors English students as well. You've exposed them to so many important literary minds, from Shakespeare to Nikki Giovanni; from Iceberg Slim to Chaucer. Your students' essays have landed them awards and scholarships. You've even been instrumental in getting our students ready for Ivy league schools."

I surveyed the room and saw each person hanging off the principal's every word. Mr. Jones had made quite the impact on everyone in the building and they were enraptured by this tribute to him. Even the lunch ladies had clasped their hands in quiet reverence. I was annoyed. None would miss him like I would.

"When I found out about this prestigious fellowship in London, I was at once ecstatic for you and sad for Coolidge. On one hand, you are young, black, and brilliant. Children all over the world—even at the Coal Hill School—need to see positive men like you. But on the other hand, we know that you are irreplaceable here at Coolidge. I can only hope that once your fellowship is over that you will be inspired to return here and teach our students all about your British adventures. We love you, we will miss you, we celebrate you, Mr. Jones!"

His eyes welled up with tears and again, I looked down at the floor. The staff applauded unrelentingly.

"Speech, speech!" shouted several teachers in the audience.

"Aw, man, you guys know I hate this…but what can I do, huh? Well I just wanted to let you all know how much I enjoyed working at Coolidge. I came here fresh out of grad school and you all welcomed me with open arms. The students have been great—a challenge, but great—and I will never forget them. But really, I couldn't have done it without all of you. You pushed me to be a better teacher and you pulled me back when I was doing too much. You helped me keep perspective. And…I don't know…I'm going to miss you. So please, come visit me in London as often as you want.

But tonight isn't about me, it's about this cake and pie we're about to crush!"

The room erupted in applause and laughter. I forced a smile and clapped as well. I looked on in envy as the folks in the room greeted and embraced Mr. Jones one at a time. I dared not join the line to steal a kiss on the cheek as many of the women in the room had.

I already knew how his stubble felt against my lips. I remembered how his face felt under my hands the first time I touched him. I blinked once, twice, three times as the old library became his living room and I remembered.

"I've been waiting for you to touch me like this…" he said.

"All night?" I asked.

"All year," he said. My hands slid from his cheeks to his neck. He shivered. I drew him close to me.

"Why didn't you say anything sooner?" I whispered in his ear.

"How was I supposed to know? You're the gym teacher. Who thinks the gym teacher likes dudes?"

"Oh so you think English teachers got the gay thing on lock?" I whispered. My lips brushed against his ear. He exhaled.

"Smith…"

"Can I kiss you, Jones?"

"Yes. Please. Kiss me, please."

I stepped back, holding him now by the shoulders. I pressed my lips against his cheek and kissed him, tracing a path from the soft mound to his warm mouth. He embraced me and parted my lips with his tongue.

I remember how sweet he tasted and how strong he smelled. Not like this musty library, whose dry odor was now punctuated with the aroma of pound cake, coconut pies, and chocolate frosting.

Memory upon memory came back, smothering me like a wool scarf. I was hot, threatening to break into a sweat. I quietly slipped out of the library and walked toward the water fountain. I pressed the button with my thumb and let the cold water splash into my mouth. I heard the clack-clack of heels coming toward me as I gulped.

"So…are you just gonna get all emotional and leave in a huff?"

I looked up to see another Old Lady Goon hovering over me.

This one was the ringleader, the supreme of the coven: Mrs. Edith Davis, the sixty-something year old, high-yellow, hazel-eyed crone. She was quite easily six feet tall but not half as scary as her sharp features or deep voice suggested.

"I'm not emotional, Mrs. Davis,"

"Look at you," she said. Well actually, she "read." Whenever she started off a sentence with "look at you" you just needed to hunker down because Mrs. Davis was about to "read you for filth" as they say, that is, tell you everything you needed to hear about yourself in that moment, even if—and especially if—it hurt your feelings.

"Look at you. Can't even stay in the same room with him to tell him a proper goodbye in front of his peers. I can't believe how far y'all fell off. I just knew this was gonna be the story for the ages, but y'all can't even get it together. You out here gulping that water like it's gonna wash away the past few years. Why don't you just man up and go back in there like a real friend would?"

"Don't you dare tell me to man up!" I spat, standing up straight and glaring at the old woman. "You don't know the half of what I've been through to keep my friendship with him. And I'd like to remind you that I'm not the one leaving the goddamn country!"

"Boy, don't you take the Lord's name in vain! Now I don't care about all this he said, he said, who-did-what first nonsense. All I know is that you are hurting, and he is hurting, and you cannot let it end like this."

"He's hurting? He's *leaving*!"

"Mr. Smith, cut it out!" Mrs. Davis said through her teeth.

I tightened my fists and loosened them again, several times over, and I silently counted slowly to ten.

"Come to Takoma Station," she commanded.

"I can't," I said firmly. Tears began to well in my eyes, but I willed them to stay in place.

"Smith, you have to. If you don't come, I promise you will regret it for the rest of your life.

"Okay, okay, shit," I relented.

"Everything is going to be okay," she said.

"I'll see you there," I responded. I walked past her, zipping up my coat while I walked past her and past the noisy library. For the briefest of moments, Jones and I locked eyes. I quickly looked away and tread down the stairs, hoping I could get myself together after a strong drink.

I parked my car on Butternut Street, the quiet, tree-lined residential street near Takoma Station Tavern, in hopes that I could muster the courage to enter and spend time with Mr. Jones one last time. As I approached the dark jazz club on my left, a DC Metrobus sped by on my right, and in the diesel stench wake of the bus, I felt myself blowing right on by like a wayward leaf. I passed all the local haunts on the block as if I'd never intended to go in at all. In seconds, I was at the very next corner. I would have walked clear into the state of Maryland if not for Cedar Street awkwardly intersecting Blair Road, creating a fortress that blocked my path. I took that as a sign from God that I should just enter Evolve, a vegan soul-food restaurant right in front of me, rather than turning around and going into Takoma Station.

I floated to the bar and "Scotch on the rocks" somehow spilled out of my mouth and into the ears of the handsome man who managed the libations. I presumed him to be my age in spite of his baby face. My grandmother as well as my mother always said, "black don't crack," so I knew I might as well add seven to ten years to whatever age I thought someone might be.

He was beyond handsome, though. He was quite sexy. Clean-shaven from scalp to chin, his broad shoulders and chest filled out his royal blue collared shirt, which was rolled up at the sleeves. He even wore a navy blue and gold paisley necktie. He was much more put-together than the bartenders elsewhere in the neighborhood, who seemed to feel that a black t-shirt and black Dickies pants were professional enough for the task of pouring drinks.

The bartender smiled at me as he carefully placed my drink in front of me. I grinned back and thought about all the things we could do in the broom closet on his lunchbreak.

I snapped back into reality and sipped my drink long and hard, damning myself for my inability to stop being a ho for even fifteen minutes. That's the shit that Mr. Jones hated—that this trail of niggas from my late teens all the way to my early thirties followed behind me like Pigpen's cloud of dust in the Charlie Brown cartoons.

I looked at the bottom of my glass into the brown liquid and then around at the bar. It was amazing how they threw a restaurant here, buttressed against the edge of the Metro station, across from a sad, but reliable liquor store. It seemed that anyone in DC could pursue their restaurateur dreams as long as they had some exposed brick and distressed chairs. That was what they called "décor" in 21st Century Washington.

But it was acceptable as far as neighborhood establishments went. Smaller than Takoma Station, and with no music, of course, but decent enough for running away from seeing the man I loved enjoy his last night with friends.

When we dated, we dated well. We drank, we ate, we loved each other the same way any other couple would. I was fearless when I was with him. I wasn't raised to be that kind of guy, though. My boyfriends were secret affairs, by and large, with other men who were just shy of being ashamed to love another man. There were track teammates in college. There were professional athletes. There were internet hookups which became committed. There were app hookups which became committed. But I wasn't the kind of guy who could change my Facebook status. And neither were they.

Plus, I was a teacher. My biggest fear was to be falsely accused of some impropriety or another against one of my students, and even though we were in the years after Ellen, Elton, and any number of gay superstars, the communities in which I worked were dens of gossip and salacious storytelling. There's no way that I would be exempt from such stories. So it made far more sense professionally to just keep my business private. I wasn't closeted. I was just meticulous in my discretion.

By my second scotch on the rocks, I was feeling the same way I felt when Mr. Jones first touched my hand. We were having a drink—not here, but up the street at Republic, a restaurant specializing in oysters.

"You sure like them fruity drinks," I teased.

"This?" he replied, pointing to the dark pink concoction before him, wrinkling his face in confusion.

"Yeah, that shit. What is that, cotton candy?" I laughed. He rolled his eyes.

"I bet you can't handle it," he said. I leaned in, speaking up over the din of the crowded bar.

"I bet I *can* handle it," I said near his ear. I leaned back. His cheeks, sandy brown though they were, flushed red. He looked at me over his glasses, as he had many times that summer in response to one of my corny jokes.

"Try it," he said, sliding the glass toward me. I blinked, grabbed the glass, then took a few gulps.

"Slow!" he said, grabbing the glass while I chugged. His fingers touched mine, stopping me from chugging—because suddenly I couldn't stop smiling. I put the glass down on the bar and continued smiling at him. Suddenly, I felt the sensation of dry, prickly cotton filling my throat and sinuses. My smile slowly but surely eroded into a grimace.

"Sneaks up on you, doesn't it?" he said. I nodded vigorously.

"What the hell is this?" I gasped.

"It's their version of a Sazerac. That's that absinthe getting you!" he laughed.

"Oh God," I said, beginning to laugh and smile again. He covered his mouth and laughed with me. I reached out to his hand and removed it from his face.

"I'm going to just take your word for it next time," I said. I placed his hand on the bar but continued to hold it. We got quiet.

"What's that for?" he asked, nodding toward our hands but still not letting go.

"Two reasons," I explained. "First, because you shouldn't cover your mouth when you laugh. You've got a smile to die for."

He blushed and his shoulders tensed up, but he never stopped smiling.

"And the second reason is because I wanted to know if you felt the same way I did," I said.

"And how do you feel?" he asked.

"I feel like I'm digging you," I replied.

"Oh yeah? Well how do you know I feel the same way?"

"Because you haven't let go of my hand yet," I said. I brought his hand to my lips and quickly kissed it. Then I let go.

His mouth hung open. He may have found my move to have been one of the slickest pimp moves of all time—and to be fair, it ranked pretty far up there—but truth be told, the long mirror behind the bar showed me where each and every person's attention was drawn. From the bartender to the young white couples all around, nobody was checking for us, so the time was right to take a chance at a public display of affection for a man I knew would appreciate it.

My bet paid off and we spent the rest of the day and night together, only coming up for air the next morning when we came back to Republic for brunch.

Our love was centered from Butternut Street to Cedar Street, along Carroll Street to Carroll Avenue, from 4th Street Market to Busboys & Poets to the US Post Office on Laurel Avenue. We owned the whole city, but Takoma was our town.

How did we get here, though? How did I get to my third Scotch on the rocks when my man was just 150 feet away with his Old Lady Goons?

Because I was a fucking coward.

Hours passed and I lost track of how much I'd had to drink, but the mystical bartender decided to begin sliding me glasses of water to drink after he pretended not to hear my call for additional alcohol. I get the hint, Magical Mister Bartender, I need to get my life together. I scrolled through my phone in an effort to sober up.

Inane text messages from former flings.

HEY STRANGER
YOU CAN'T TALK TO NOBODY NO MORE?
I RODE PAST TAKOMA, I SEEN YOU IN THERE LOOKING ALL DEPRESSED AT THE BAR

I sighed and deleted them all without responding.

I went through my dating apps. Dozens of notifications in the past few hours of just being at the bar, discoverable to anyone within miles who was also using the apps.

I was disgusted. At them. At myself. At my cowardice.

YOU AIN'T SHIT FOR MISSING THIS HAPPY HOUR, SMITH!

My heart sank to read the message from Mrs. Washington's text.

Y'ALL STILL THERE? I asked.

NO, WE JUST LEFT! JONES WENT HOME! ASSHOLE! she replied.

I'MA MAKE IT RIGHT, WASHINGTON. DON'T HATE ME.

BYE.

I had to face him, even if I didn't want to be faced. I motioned for the bartender and I gave him a wad of cash.

"Keep the change," I said, my eyes half-closed.

"Thanks man. You gonna be okay getting home?" he asked.

"Yeah. I'ma walk to my friend's place. He's only a block from here."

"Oh…you not talking about Mr. Jones, are you? Slim dude? Dreadlocks?"

"How you know that?"

"I used to see y'all together all the time. I mean, not to be in your business. But y'all were the kings of Takoma for a while there. I always wondered what happened when I stopped seeing you around here. And I gotta say…nah, never mind. Not my place."

"What? Tell me."

"Well…I ain't never seen two happier people. And you looked a lot happier then than you do right now. Say man, you sure you'll be alright?"

"Yeah. I'm good. Thanks." I was annoyed at the Magical Sexy Bartender, but he was right. I was miserable. Miserable and tipsy.

I zipped up my leather coat and dug my hands into the pockets. It got colder out, and I braced myself for the chilly air hitting me as I walked the block to the small apartment building where Mr. Jones lived. For that year and a half he and I were together—one summer, one school year, and one more summer—his place was my place and my place was his place. When we felt like being Petworth hipster trash, bouncing from used bookstore to funky sushi bar, we stayed at my place, a sleek upper level, two-bedroom apartment over the metro station at Georgia Avenue. There, we watched high definition action movies on my 60-inch 4k television. We made exotic drinks at my kitchen bar. We fucked like rabbits in every room, and sometimes late at night on the roof.

And when we felt like being black bohemians, we returned to Takoma, walking the half mile between his cozy apartment with hardwood floors and bay windows to the bead store, where he'd purchase the occasional cowrie shells to weight down his stray dreadlocks. We'd listen—on vinyl, if he could help it, to Nina Simone, John Coltrane, and David Bowie. I cringed when he'd put on Bowie, but he insisted I'd love him some day.

We had already broken up by the time David Bowie died. I had been visiting fraternity brothers in New York that weekend and got on an early train back to DC. Still hungover, I couldn't believe what I was reading on social media: David Bowie had died of cancer. What the fuck? I immediately thought of Jones. But it was like four in the morning. I couldn't just wake him up out of his sleep to tell him the news. But it was all over social media. Was that going to be how he found out? Did he even want to hear from me at all?

I looked on his Facebook page every half-hour on the trip back to DC. Would he wake up? Would he see? Would he post? I should send him a message…

But I didn't. My train pulled into DC just after 8am. I could have switched from the Amtrak to the Red line, but who could trust the Red line on a Monday morning? There were always breakdowns and track work and some schmuck deciding to off himself in the middle of the commute. I caught an Uber to work instead and I got to the school before the first bell sounded. I clocked in and ran up to the third floor, to Jones' room.

Breathing hard, I peered in the glass window of the door, reinforced with wire mesh. Jones was seated away from the door in his black swivel chair. I slowly opened the door and heard a tinny version of "Starman" piercing the otherwise silent classroom. Jones' cell phone laid on a stack of ungraded papers on his desk while he buried his face in the palms of his hands. His back, draped by his long hair, heaved up and down in small bursts.

"Mr. Jones?" I asked.

"Yeah," he said, quickly straightening up his body in his seat while he wiped away the tears. He turned himself to face me. I guess the concern in my face was so grave that he just needed to break down all over again. He sobbed, big gasping sobs of abject grief.

"Hey, it's okay," I said. I hurried to him as he stood up. I touched his shoulder, unsure what he wanted me to do. He tried to avoid looking at me, perhaps so I wouldn't notice his red eyes and nose, but I didn't care. He was hurt, so I hurt.

I grabbed him and pulled him toward me in a tight embrace. He sobbed. My eyes watered.

"It's okay," I repeated. "He was your hero."

"I knew he wouldn't live forever. But I wasn't ready."

"I know. I know."

I stroked his hair while I held him. The first bell would ring shortly and we'd both have to get it together soon, but in this moment, being there for him emotionally and physically was all I needed. I couldn't bring David Bowie back, but I could be his rock in that terrible moment.

And in the minutes it took me to walk to his apartment, I had replayed that moment over and over, the last time I really held him.

I called him on my cell phone.

"Hey."

"Let me in."

"You outside?"

"Yeah."

"Why?"

"Just let me in. Please."

He hung up. I looked up. Two flights above me were two identical bay windows. The one on the right was Jones'. In about a minute, he appeared in the doorway, letting me in.

"Hi," I said softly.

"Hey." I walked past him and started walking up the stairs. He followed.

"I guess I thought I'd never see you again," he said.

"Yeah, I'm sorry I didn't come to Takoma Station. That wasn't the right move on my part." I tried to stay cool. I hated apologies.

"Why didn't you come?"

Ugh, the probing questions. He could never just take anyone at face value. He wanted to know how all the moving parts worked, whether he was spending all day watching Congressional hearings on C-SPAN or interrogating me about my feelings.

I put my hand on his doorknob and turned it. Locked.

"I got it," he said. "Been a few thefts in the building lately, so I can't be too careful." He stood in front of me and put his key in the lock. His head right in front of me, I bent over and inhaled. He still smelled like that mix of coconut oil and a faint trace of his favorite cologne. He took half a step back and bumped into me.

"Sorry," he said. He pushed the door open and I followed him through, staying just as close as I had been in the hallway. Just as I heard the door swing shut, I hugged him from behind.

"You're drunk," he sniped. I let him go and spun him around. I leaned down to his face and sniffed, once, then twice.

"You don't smell like someone who just came from an AA meeting yourself," I retorted. He clasped my chin and looked up at me.

"You don't govern my alcohol intake," he said. He released my chin and his hand slid down my chest. My heart began to race.

"You nervous?" he asked. He unzipped my jacket while I stood frozen.

"Yes," I said. He gently folded my jacket in half the long way and tossed it over the edge of his sofa.

"Why?" He rubbed his hands over my chest, my abs, my arms.

"Because I miss you. And I love you. And I don't want to hurt you anymore. That's why I stayed away from Takoma Station. I didn't want to disrupt--"

"Stop talking," he said. He grabbed my hand and led me into his dark bedroom. I could barely see, but I knew him—and this room—well enough to know about a week's worth of clothes were strewn about the floor. I'd need to tread lightly so I wouldn't fall.

Through the window blinds, which were half open, the light from the streetlamp cast ghostly shadows amid fluorescent orange beams of light that my eyes slowly adjusted to.

He let go of my hand and walked to his side of the bed,

closest to the window. Well, it was all his bed, but it was his side when I was there. My side was near the closet. I felt my way to the nightstand and took off my watch and my rings. I slipped out of my boots and felt myself shrink about an inch. I unbuttoned my shirt and removed my belt. My pants sagged low on my hips, held up only by the muscular thighs I prided myself on as a runner.

Jones took off his glasses and peeled off his sweater. He left on a leather bracelet. He was toned under his bulky clothes—slender, but well defined. He undid his belt buckle and his pants fell to the ground, revealing snug boxer briefs. They were probably black. He was unpredictable in many respects: temperament, career, political opinions. But when it came to his fundamentals, he could always be depended upon for black underwear, eyeglasses (rather than contact lenses), and vinyl records.

"Come here," I said.

"No," he said. He slid his hands behind his neck. Slowly, he rubbed himself from the sides of his neck, down his chest, across his abs, and down under the waistband of his underwear, where they stayed in defiance. I knelt on the bed and leaned forward on my hands, now on all fours.

"Come here…please…" I asked.

"You know what I want to hear, Tony," he said, sliding his underwear down to the floor. I crawled toward his erect penis until I was an inch from it.

"Akachi," I said.

"That's right. Say my name."

"Akachi. Akachi Jones." I kissed his inner thigh, repeating his first name with every peck landed, moistening my lips the closer I got to his manhood.

Akachi Jones was a black gay man who taught with me at Calvin Coolidge High School in Northwest Washington, DC. I was attracted to him the moment I saw him on the first day of school for teachers in August of 2013. His dreadlocks, back then, were just sweeping his shoulders. I found him hard to get to know that first year, partially because he was an introvert, but partially because my work in the physical education department took place clear across the building in the gymnasium, while his English classes were exclusively held in the dark corners of the third floor.

From time to time, I'd try to sit near him at staff meetings, but he was surrounded by his friends, older ladies who taught in various departments. On one hand, I didn't care who knew that I was gay—outside of the building. Inside, I preferred keeping my private affairs confidential. Because of this discretion, however, I had no way of knowing Mr. Jones' backstory.

As luck would have it, Akachi Jones and I were both selected to serve as co-directors of the Ward 4 day camp, held at Coolidge in 2014. All eight wards of the city would have one anchor day camp to provide enrichment and remediation activities for elementary and middle school students. Yeah, it was mostly summer school and free meals for poor children in disguise. From June to August, we worked in the hot building, teaching academic subjects during the morning and leading cultural and recreational activities in the afternoon, all while making sure the students were well-fed and safe.

I admired his work ethic. He truly put the students first in everything he did. He wasn't the aloof introvert I thought he was, at least when it came to the kids. He smiled when he taught. He made Shakespeare cool. He drew connections between hip-hop and British literature that I never thought would work—but it did, for the kids. I even saw him hilariously try, and fail, to introduce David Bowie music to his students. *Maybe one day*, I told him.

I thought I saw signals, but I wasn't sure. Our relationship became close, built on professional trust, but then evolved into flirtation. Bromance was evolving into romance, so it seemed. The pat on the back. The playful teasing.

After a particularly long week, we went for drinks at Republic and I made my move. My heart skipped beats and my stomach did flips, but I knew I had to do something, to say something, to make sure that what I was feeling went beyond attraction.

The first night was like our last night and our last night was like right now. I tasted every inch of him. I grabbed him. I wrapped his hair around my hand, and I pulled him. I pleased him. He dominated me. And vice versa. We made love. And that's how I knew.

Perhaps we were too close, too soon, but the ensuing year was the best year of my life, with the best man I knew. I loved him. I was in love with him. Mine was his. His was mine. Even my mom liked him, and she don't like nobody.

I listened to him as he explained his fears to me, but I dismissed them. "I'm not like those other dudes," I said. "I'm not going anywhere."

I listened to him as he shared his insecurities about being the son of an African woman and a white man, how on some days he felt black. Like, black-black. Like he belonged here. He felt in the mix of the Black Lives Matter movement. His heart ached when Trayvon Martin was killed. He wept with his students when one of their own was taken by neighborhood violence. He felt like this community was where he belonged.

But I also listened when he said he didn't feel black. Growing up was bad. He fit neither here nor there and often had to make do on his own. White kids knew he wasn't white. Black kids might have known he was black, but he was so light, so very light, that it was impossible for him to merely fit in.

He had his baggage, but I promised to protect him.

The year passed and we decided to tell the Old Lady Goon Squad that we were together. I wasn't afraid of them. I didn't care who knew. But I was glad that they approved of us.

The summer of 2015 went by, and one by one, our house of cards came crashing down. I was haunted by the ghosts of relationships past. Seems like not a weekend went by without some throwback son of a bitch calling me or texting me, asking where I was at and could I meet up with them.

Akachi Jones was not normally a jealous man, but I suppose the frequency of the messages I was receiving and the nonchalant way I was handling them made him insecure. He became moody, needed time alone, wanted to spend some time apart. Not a lot, but just enough to recharge.

I resented him for it. And instead of taking the time to reassess my next move—which ought to have been an engagement ring—I let some old flame come to my apartment and give me a blow job. I didn't kiss him. I barely hugged him. But I did let him suck my dick.

Of course Akachi found out. I don't have a password on my phone because I had no reason to think anyone would ever want to see it. But Akachi did. He found texts. He found all types of guys trying to get at me and he did find the guy who had sucked me off.

He was done. There was no going back from that moment. I said I was sorry, but I didn't really mean it. I was sorry he found out, sure. But I don't know a single dude who would turn down head—head you knew was gonna be good—from anybody.

I thought we'd find our way back to each other once the school year got rolling again, but it was too late. I'd been frozen out. Even the Old Lady Goon squad barely eked out an icy "hello" if they saw me in the halls.

He let me in when David Bowie died in January 2016. We worked on our friendship again from there, but mainly in the school building. He was still hurt, but he wasn't as angry. Spring became summer and time went on. I missed my man, but I didn't know how to get him back. The ship had seemingly sailed.

I slipped my underwear and jeans back on when our lovemaking session ended. He did the same. It was cold in his apartment—too cold to be sitting around naked, even after a good fucking.

I left the bed and walked out of the room.

"You leaving?" he called out.

"Naw, just getting some water," I said back. I heard him get out of bed and follow me. I grabbed a cup off the top of his refrigerator and filled it with filtered water from the front of the stainless-steel icebox. I gulped it. He leaned on the kitchen island and stared at me.

"What happened to us?" I asked him, wiping my mouth. His entire countenance changed from ease to annoyance.

"What happened to us?" He stood up straight. "Mike happened to us. And after Mike, Jason happened to us. Who *didn't* happen to us, Tony? You were never fully invested in me, not once. There was always someone else who had a piece of you."

"Those are exes."

"They didn't seem like it. You didn't act like it.... I made the mistake of thinking I could ever be enough for you."

"You are enough."

"I was never enough."

"You were too much! Too much for me. Then, at least. Too good to be true."

"You know how many times a man has told me that, Tony? My sophomore year in college, I liked this guy—white guy, matter of fact—and I am thinking wow, I like a white dude. I'm gonna shoot my shot and see what he says. I told him I wanted to take him out. You know what he said? 'I know you want something serious, Akachi. You don't want somebody like me. I'm not serious enough for you.'"

"Akachi, you're the most intense person I know."

"I can't help who I am!"

"I'm not saying it's a bad thing. At all. I like you how you are. I love it. I just didn't know how to handle you then."

"And I guess I didn't know how to handle you, either, playa."

"Don't call me a player."

"But aren't you, though? That dude my sophomore year…he was right. I needed somebody serious. And I guess I just never found him. Time after time, I fall into these…these…situations with dudes. Never quite meeting the level of relationship."

"We were together well over a year. Don't try to ret-con our relationship."

"Judging by all the men in your phone, it's hard to believe we were in a relationship. You did me wrong just like everyone else ever has."

"I tried, Akachi. I tried, and I wasn't perfect, but I loved you the best way I could. But you know what your problem is? You think you're entitled to a Prince Charming. You are a damn good person and I love you, but me loving you ain't enough to make *me* perfect. I love you enough to try, but when are you going to try for me? You judge me against a long line of niggas I don't even know. You give me one strike and I'm out of there. You ignored me for months. You don't give me the chance to make it up to you. You don't give me the chance to *try*. All I ever wanted to do was try, but you froze me out."

Akachi walked away from the kitchen and I followed him toward the living room. Intense conversations with him were surreal, like I was watching a movie of myself having a real, grown-up conversation.

"I just couldn't stand another heartbreak. I needed to let you go before…"

"Before what?" I asked.

"Before I couldn't let go at all."

"Come here," I demanded.

"No."

"Come here," I insisted.

"Leave me alone," he said.

"Akachi. Please." He looked at me through his glasses and exhaled. He slowly walked to me. Stopping about a foot away from my face, he looked down at our naked feet, his pale toes like talons on his hardwood floor, and mine like brown and gray sausage links.

"You ashy," he said.

"You need to cut your toenails. Look at me. Don't go."

"Don't do this."

"You don't have to go. You can still decline. They have a wait list, I'm sure of it."

"Smith--"

"You know how many teachers are dying to work overseas?"

"Yes! I'm one of them! I need to do this, Smith."

"And I need you! Akachi, never in my life have I needed someone the way I need you. I love you. I like you. You are my best friend and there will never be anyone else like you. I can't imagine a day in my life where you aren't in it. Can you honestly tell me that you can go to England and forget about me?"

"I could never forget about you, Tony. The time we spent together was beautiful. You make me feel…like…like really happy to be a *man.* When you're growing up totally unsure of yourself, uncomfortable in your own family and community, not sure if who you are is who you're supposed to be, then going to college and still not finding anyone like you…it's a real downer, man. It makes for a really shaky start to your adulthood. But when I met you, I was taken by your confidence. Your swagger. Your absolute and total disregard for what the fuck people thought of you. And to think somebody so confident, so handsome, so sexy…to think that he wanted me? That he still wants me? That's not only flattering, that's humbling. I see your sincerity, Tony. I see it in the creases of your frown and the darkness in your eyes. I know you're for real. I don't want to believe it, but I know it. And maybe deep down I'm just scared that somebody like you could love somebody like me so hard.

How could I ever live up to that? Maybe it's just easier for me to be mad because somebody else loved you, too. Maybe it was just easier for me to cut you off so that I couldn't get hurt any worse than I already was. Yeah, you hurt me, Tony. But you ain't hurt me that bad. It was just feeling like the same old black gay song and dance that we've all played before. I thought you were just like everyone else I've dated. But I see how wrong I was. I love you, Tony. And I'm really going to miss you, man."

"So there's really no changing your mind, huh? No matter how hard I fight?"

"I've really messed things up. I should have been fighting, too. For you. For us. Maybe I would have stayed another year. Maybe we could have been taking this trip together."

"Me? Go to England?"

"It would probably be the only way I could convince you to finally give David Bowie a listen."

"I listen to David Bowie!"

"Yeah, but not for real," Akachi said. He walked away from me and toward his stereo and turntable.

"You think David Bowie was 'Space Oddity' and 'Changes' and red eyeshadow and flamboyant outfits."

"Well…wasn't he?"

"Yeah, but he was also a little funk…a little soul. Check it out." He carefully removed the vinyl disc from the sleeve and placed it on the turntable. He handed me the cover. *Young Americans* was the album.

Once we were lovers
Can they understand?

The mid-tempo ballad blared from his speakers and he took the cover from my hand.

"Can I have this dance?" he asked. I nodded and softly placed my arms around him. We moved side to side, out of pace with the rhythm, but on-speed with David Bowie's croon. He turned his head to the side while we moved, resting on my chest.

Can you hear me?
Can you feel me inside?

I felt my shirt get wet with his tears. I kissed the top of his head and slowly rubbed his back.

"It's okay," I whispered.

"I'm sorry," he said. "I'm just really going to miss you."

I let go of him and stepped back. He wiped his eyes.

"Oh God, don't look at me like this," he said.

I smiled.

"You will always be perfect to me."

He laughed.

"Snot and all, huh?"

"Especially the snot," I said. "But maybe you want a Kleenex anyway?"

We laughed even more. I led him to his sofa, where a box of tissue waited for him on the coffee table. He grabbed a few and blew his nose.

I took my cell phone from my back pocket and sat on the sofa, leaning back.

"Let me hold you," I said. He balled up the tissue and tossed it into a nearby trash can.

"Okay," he said. He laid down on top of me and slowly exhaled as he settled in. He took his glasses off and laid them on the table. I massaged his scalp while he rested. I never had dreadlocks a day in my life and had never been with a man who'd had them, either. Akachi was so free with himself, at least when I was with him, that I could explore his body like I was his child. I smelled him. I tasted him. I touched him. I gazed at him when he was naked, when he knew I was looking and when he didn't. I watched the way he chewed his food. I watched how he stood when he pissed. I felt his scalp through his new growth just underneath the part of the dreadlock where it wasn't tightly matted together. His hair texture was soft in that place. I couldn't run my fingers through it, but I could rub his scalp and massage it in small circles.

I raised my free hand and scrolled through my apps. Akachi's body now rose and fell with the rhythm of a sleeping man. I clicked on TripAdvisor.

Cheap Flights.

One Way.

Washington, DC – All Airports.

London, United Kingdom – All Airports.

Departure? I don't know, let's just say January 10.

$439 from Dulles Airport? Not bad. I'll take it.

Purchase.

My phone buzzed in my hand from the various notifications of a successful purchase. I now had less than a month to quit my job, pack my shit, figure out whether I needed a visa, and to somehow tell the love of my life that I wasn't going to let him go that easily. He might yell at me. He might cuss me out in his own special way—how he couldn't really say "mufucka" or "goddamn" – but always a hard *er* on motherfucker and a hard *ed* on goddamned. And his little light brown nose might wrinkle up as he's cussing and pointing his slim finger at me.

But all I will do is smile and laugh at him, infuriating him further. Because this time, I am going to fight for the both of us—and we are going to win.

FLOATING IN A MOST PECULIAR WAY:

HOW DAVID BOWIE SET ME FREE
2016

In Dardenland, there are two running truths:

1. Lenny Kravitz is my husband.
2. David Bowie is my father.

For some reason, it's readily understood among my friends and acquaintances that Lenny is my husband; he belongs to me and there is little dissension about that. (Perhaps because I acknowledge everyone else's imaginary baes and don't try to claim them.) It's to the point where anytime Lenny Kravitz is on television, I get a good five or six messages or tags notifying me. Sometimes it gets so annoying that I wish I never married him.

Not so easily acceptable is when I tell people David Bowie is my father. The response is usually a quizzical look followed by "If David Bowie is your father, then who is your mother?" Well my mother is my mother, dummy! You met her!

Of course David Bowie is not really my father. No matter how much I wished it were so, it was not. My father never claimed me, didn't want me, and is not interested in a relationship with me even now. It is not a unique story and doesn't warrant further explanation: he is a deadbeat.

Somewhere in my childhood, I came to terms with the fact that the man to whom I owe half my DNA would not eventually come around. I honestly don't recall a whole lot of yearning and depression, though there was sadness and disappointment. As an only child, I somehow got over the absence and filled the void with books, movies, and music. Even as I write this, I recall watching *Entertainment Tonight* with my family and keeping up with pop culture that way.

So it must have been *Entertainment Tonight* that first introduced me to the upcoming film *Labyrinth*. It had everything I needed. At that time, everything I needed was the Muppets and anything related to Jim Henson, who himself was a fatherly demi-god to me.

On *Entertainment Tonight*, I remember the fuss they raised about this man playing The Goblin King. "Rocker David Bowie" was how he was usually described.

This early images from *Labyrinth* were amazing. By the time I saw the Shaft of Hands, I was sold.

Mommy, we HAVE to see Labyrinth.

And we did.

Unlike many fans, I did not fall in love with David Bowie in a romantic sense then, and I am not in love with David Bowie now. I've never been sexually attracted to him. Not even once, generous package in *Labyrinth* be damned.

What I saw on the silver screen was The Goblin King: a flamboyantly masculine, magical ruler who lived at the center of an impossible puzzle. He wore makeup, carried a cane, and led a band of misfit goblins. He wore shiny things and played with shiny things, just like me. I've never owned a G.I. Joe but ask me how many crystals and prisms I played with well before *Labyrinth.*

He was larger than life. I was here for all of it.

As far as films go, *Labyrinth* appealed my eight-year-old sensibilities. Although I had friends and was well-liked, I always felt different. An outsider on the inside. I liked a lot of things my friends had no particular awareness of, and *Labyrinth* only widened the differences. The film made me delve deeper into fantasy literature, such as *A Wrinkle in Time.* I was exposed to the art of M.C. Escher. I fell in love with the acrobatics of Michael Moschen. And of course, *Labyrinth* was my gateway drug to the music of David Bowie.

Labyrinth came out in 1986. For the next three years I listened to the vinyl album over and over and watched the VHS tape practically every weekend. I wish I had kept count of how many times I've seen it. Perhaps not that many, but it sure feels like hundreds.

Through dangers untold and hardships unnumbered…

Sound + Vision came out in 1989, when I was ten. By then, VH1 had done its part to make sure I was caught up with all the Bowie music videos I could possibly fall in love with: *China Girl*, *Let's Dance,* and *Modern Love* were favorites. *Jazzin' for Blue Jean*, the long form music video for "Blue Jean" was also really good. And perhaps by then, the film *Absolute Beginners* had begun playing on DC's channel 20.

In those three years, I was as fully indoctrinated as I could be, as a relatively poor kid who couldn't buy his own music. When *Sound + Vision* came out, my body was ready.

While I don't think I cried when I opened my Christmas gifts and found this three-cassette transparent box, I do remember utter elation. I had no idea what I was going to hear, but I knew it would be pure excellence.

Now, had anyone in my family known what this box set was *supposed* to be, they would not have gotten it for me. *Sound + Vision* was, and remains, a treat for the fans. The vast majority of the collection is B-sides, demos, and alternate takes on classic tracks. For example, the version of "The Prettiest Star" found here is a previously unreleased mono take (which remains my favorite version). Another example is an all-German version of "Heroes," called "Helden" here.

I largely listened to *Sound + Vision* on a Walkman. Listening to the opening sounds of "Station to Station" in my ear sent chills through my body. I thought that train was somehow right behind me. And "Warszawa" remains a chilling song I'd rather not even listen to. That's how weird and evocative it was, yet I still loved it. I loved every last track on those tapes to death.

Before *Sound + Vision*, my love for all things David Bowie was quirky, but still mainstream, as everything I knew of him was family-friendly, or at the very least, appropriate for daytime viewing on VH1 and local television. After *Sound + Vision*, I felt changed. This love wasn't just about *Labyrinth* anymore. I had listened to a genius.

Had I been less possessive of my things, I might have loaned the tapes out to share this experience with my friends. But really, who among them would be receptive? I knew I was listening to bona fide rock and roll. The closest my friends got to this kind of music was Madonna, George Michael, and Peter Gabriel–again, thank you VH1. In reality, the rest of my circle was being turned out by hip-hop and go-go, genres I would not appreciate until I was practically an adult. In the meantime, I'd just have to appreciate David Bowie by myself.

I read up on David Bowie as much as I could over the next few years. I read the liner notes to *Sound + Vision* religiously as well as any articles I could find. Somehow, I found out about his ex-wife Angie and his son, Zowie Bowie (really [and thankfully] named Duncan Jones). By the time David Bowie got married to Iman in 1992, I was an expert. (I probably was not, but who was gonna check me? Literally nobody else I knew listened to him.)

Much has been written about how David Bowie represents outsiders through his craft, and it is all true. He was at once queer and straight, masculine and feminine, refined and otherworldly. He was rock and roll, surely, but he was also soul–and I suppose that sound, as well as the occasional background vocals by Luther Vandross, is what drew me in.

Rumors had swirled about Luther's sexual orientation for years and my household was not immune to such gossip. Add to that narrative David Bowie's admitted (if not exaggerated) bisexuality, my young mind crafted a story in which David Bowie had turned out Luther Vandross and now they were just good friends. How I got there, I don't know, but it's a story that seemed natural to my emerging, imminently queer mind.

I had deep emotions for boys at a pretty young age. I remember being in first grade at Bunker Hill Elementary School, gazing upon a beautiful third grader playing across the asphalt yard, and thinking to myself "I'm in love with a boy." Chalk it up to the Cancerian sensitivity or the melodramatics of what was on television at the time (*Dynasty, Dallas*, et al), but that's what I really thought–that I had fallen into impossible, devastating love with someone of my own gender.

I buried those feelings deep inside and hoped they'd go away, even as I got drawn deeper and deeper into the Bowie mystique.

At a certain age, perhaps 12 or 13, I realized that when I masturbated, I was thinking of my pastor's stepson. There was no going back: I was gay. Well, at the time, I convinced myself that I was really bisexual *just like David Bowie,* and everything would eventually be okay. If Bowie could marry Iman, then maybe I could marry a woman someday, too.

It wasn't until I reached college that I realized that bisexual thing was just a stepping-stone, but thank you David Bowie for getting me there safely, with thoughts of suicide only creeping into my head once, and that was only after a terrible relationship my senior year–not because I felt I wouldn't be accepted or because God didn't love me.

Oh no love! You're not alone.

I was largely late to the Bowie party compared to the rest of the fandom, entering into what most believe was his lowest point creatively–that terrible decade called the 1980s. But for me, it was a golden age. As written above, I got to dive head-first into *Sound + Vision*, and soon after, *The Singles Collection*, aka *The Singles 1969 to 1993*. With the *Singles Collection*, I was finally able to have in my possession the "real versions" of the songs that were demos and remixes on *Sound + Vision*. I definitely wore those cassette tapes out. I brought them to school and finally shared them with friends. I was in junior high school by then, and even though we were in the midst of a great wave of urban music, I did inject some rock into my friends' lives.

I should note that the only recollection I have of the album *Black Tie White Noise* album, which also came out in 1993, was the single "Jump They Say." Loved the song, hated the video–didn't want to see my hero playing around with the concept of death.

1995 is when I began purchasing my own Bowie albums when they came out–with my own damn money from summer and after school jobs. I felt like a grown-up and this is perhaps why the later years are my favorite Bowie era.

Outside, Earthling, "Hours…," Heathen, Reality… all of these albums were the soundtrack to my life as I came into my own as a student, as a man, and as a novelist.

So many tributes will be written in this vein, so I will add only the following pieces of trivia:

In my first novel, ***Lazarus***, there is a scene in which Adrian Collins, who is pledging a fraternity, has to give a special greeting to one of the alumni brothers. Since Adrian is the best singer on the pledge line, so hearing him deliver the greeting is a special treat. The Brother? Big Brother Sound & Vision.

"Don't you wonder sometiiiiiiiimes….'bout sound and visionnnn?"

There may be other Bowie Easter eggs in my writing–the tributes are practically subconscious at this point.

Additionally, I create music playlists for each of my novels. "Fame" is a sort of theme song for Adrian Collins in *Covenant*, as he is fresh off the "burning sands" for his fraternity and reclaims his title as "Big Man on Campus." "It's Gonna Be Me" is a love song for Adrian and his eventual boyfriend, varsity basketball player Isaiah Aiken.

Several Bowie tracks are also on the soundtrack of *Epiphany*, including "We All Go Through" from *'Hours…'* and "Right" from *Young Americans*. There is not a novel I've written without the help of a David Bowie song or two.

His final single "Lazarus" is also the name of my first novel. Even though I know he wasn't reading my novels for inspiration, it's nice that we have this one small thing in common.

When David Bowie had his heart attack in 2004, I was convinced that he would be retired from music for good. The re-releases, compilations, and box sets kept coming, but the new music was nowhere to be seen. Although I did really want new releases, somewhere deep in my heart I wanted him to just chill and be a dad and a husband.

Isn't that weird? This was a man I did not know personally, but for some reason I was like "Nah, we good. Take care of that baby."

In the meantime, I delved even deeper into his earlier music, even before *Space Oddity*. While I continue to work on new novels, "Love You Till Tuesday" and "In The Heat of the Morning" from the deluxe edition of *David Bowie* have been playing on an eternal loop in my head. There are times where I envision my main characters holding each other in bed while they listen to this album.

Perhaps I needed a decade away from Bowie to be able to appreciate the totality of his career and his message. I definitely needed that decade to appreciate what are perhaps his greatest albums, *The Next Day* and *Blackstar*.

In that time, I reached a certain level of peace about having a father who does not love me. I had used every means at my disposal to reach him and other members of my family, but they were fruitless–until I met my half-brother. I am proud that he and I have begun and maintained a relationship. The fact that I don't have a relationship with my father is now just a fact of my life. I'm no longer angry about it. I'm no longer sad.

David Bowie was never my father, either. But how fun it was to pretend that I could be the offspring of the most fabulous man in the universe. Here was a man who made it cool to be different. He was a man who thumbed his nose at binaries. There was never anything "either/or" about David Bowie. It was always "everything" and "here's some more."

I imagine that one day David Bowie decided he could have it all, and he did. I had a similar revelation a few years ago, too. And why not? Why not devote my life to the things that make me happy?

I never feel perfect–but I do feel successful. And when I don't feel successful, I know that it's okay because it's not over yet. In all of those times, my ups and my downs, the formative years and the later years, the music of David Bowie has gotten me through. He wasn't my dad, but his music was loyal, even when it was ever changing.

Indeed, I learned from David Bowie how to be free. How to be good. How to be okay. How to find within myself the tools that I needed when I couldn't find them from anyone else.

I could be a Thin White Duke. I could be the Goblin King. I could marry well. I could be imperfect all my life while still being great.

I could overcome. I could do terrible things in my youth and atone for them. I could turn victimhood into victory.

I could speak out for others who don't look like me or live my life.

I could create art that could survive for all time.

I am proud that the man we knew as David Bowie wrote the music that punctuated important moments in my life. How beautiful, how vast were his gifts to all of us. I am humbled by the accident, the mystery, the Divine Providence which dictated that I might live in the same time that David Bowie did; that his birth and his death and that my birth and my death would somehow exist in the same time stream so that I might somehow be influenced and forever changed by his genius.

I am overwhelmed with gratitude that I got to live at the same time as David Bowie. Yet, I am still profoundly sad that a man I jokingly called my father is now gone. There will be no more tours. There will be no more concerts. There will be no more evolution of style. A man we hoped would escape the call of the Grim Reaper has sung his final song.

I will never be the same. But God is change, so said Octavia Butler.

The man we knew as David Bowie is dead. May his gifts live on forever through us all.

At the end of the day, I don't like being told what to do.
--September 9, 2012

The Falcon Crest theme song is my alarm in the morning. I am royalty.

--August 18, 2011

PRIMORDIAL HURT: A *BEING MARY JANE* REFLECTION

2016

There was one time that I went on a tirade on my blog and said things I regretted.

It was not the time that I was investigated by DC Public Schools because of an anonymous complaint someone made about me. It seems as though calling your students "Satan's Little Helpers" on your blog is a trigger for some people in the community. I didn't regret it, though. I truly did used to teach Satan's Little Helpers. They have now leveled up to Satan's Minions.

Nor was it the time I called out a homophobic member of Alpha Phi Alpha on my blog. There was a period where Alphas across the nation felt it was their duty to tell me how despicable the so-called homosexual lifestyle was and how I had no right to write the novels I was writing and was becoming somewhat successful at. Well, when you email me your hate, you can't be mad when I copy and paste that email and publish it to my blog.

After threats to get lawyers involved, I did remove the posting, but that Brother still lost his election to public office. A decade later, he has still never been elected to public office, but I am still writing books.

No regrets there.

But I do regret how I treated a man I loved so much, that when he hurt me, I told the world that I hated him. It is not something we've been able to bounce back from, even after well over a decade since.

In or around 2005, I got a message on dating site from a handsome man with creamy brown skin named Shane Prentice. He was well-spoken but urban in presentation—straight out of a Timberland print advertisement from the era.

Even today, this is an aesthetic I prefer. As I try to understand why my vision of sexy is stuck in the year 2003, I have to think it's partly because of my addiction to nostalgia and all things slightly out of sync with modernity, as well as the idea of what manliness means. To me, nothing was manlier than baggy jeans, a baseball cap slightly cocked to the side, and a gold chain. This is how my favorite rappers still dress, and they are still sexy to me.

So this was the man I first met on the dating site. Other than the fact that he seemed to enjoy smoking marijuana, I saw enough to upgrade him from in-site messages to email conversations.

His emails to me were from his work account. Immediately, I was concerned. There was no way I could have deep conversations with this guy without his IT department potentially reading them. Why wouldn't he give me his regular email? Didn't he have one?

We exchanged numbers as well. I supposed we texted and talked a few times, but something very quickly didn't feel right.

A year later, I had met a man named Richard Stark. Rich was my fraternity brother and was the Site Director of an after-school program called Heads Up: A University-Neighborhood Initiative. I took a part-time job as a Test Literacy Instructor with Heads Up and enjoyed the extra pay for a few months. Soon, Rich asked me "Hey. Could you see yourself doing my job?" Like an extra in a Hollywood musical, I said "Do I?! Of course I do!" He told me there were positions opening up and that I should apply.

He also adamantly said he would recuse himself from the selection process and that I'd have to work for it myself.

Rich had an interesting ethical system that way. By the time I left the job, he and I were no longer friends whatsoever. For a long time, though, I felt like he was a good big brother who pushed me to be great.

On the other hand, part of being in a fraternity is to use those connections based on your own exposure to a person to help them get an extra push toward their goals, presuming they are worthy in the first place. And if they're not, your responsibility as a brother becomes the act of getting them to worthiness.

So I didn't understand Rich's recusal. But it didn't matter—I had a man on the inside that Rich didn't know about:

Shane Prentice.

Although he and I didn't necessarily stay in touch over the year since we first spoke, we were still cordial. When I scored my first interview with Denise Holloway, I let Shane know. He was overjoyed and promised to do anything he could to get me in there. It seemed as though he thought I was an even better fit than I thought myself.

And unlike Rich, Shane neither disclosed his prior relationship with me, nor did he recuse himself from the interview process. When I made it to the next round, a panel of other employees, Shane was right there.

I have always given great interviews. By the time I make it to a final round, I never bomb. The people making the hiring decisions never had to worry about my qualifications, just whether or not I'd be the right fit. I went into this particular interview with a lot of confidence.

There were three interviewers: a black guy I happened to know from college (who later became my boss—and a terrible one, at that), a white woman who was nice enough (but always seemed a tad judgmental), and Shane.

I was at ease. The questions came in rapid fire but were friendly. I made them laugh. I made them think. It was rigorous, but I had been well-prepared for the moment.

Then it came.

Out of the blue, Shane began to laugh. First a quiet tee-hee. Then a ta-ha. Then a full out guffaw. I knew what had happened in his brain: the stress of keeping up the façade that we didn't know each other finally came to a head. Right there in the middle of the meeting.

The white woman and the other black guy just stared at him for a while. Then finally the white woman asked me to excuse Shane. He apologized through the tears and the interview continued.

That night I cussed him out for almost ruining my interview. He giggled.

I ended up getting the job, as did the other top candidate in the field. Although we were competing against each other, we became great friends. We also became the very next two people to resign from the organization, after Shane. Six months after my start date, all three of us were gone.

Somewhere after the time I stopped giving Shane the time of day as a potential suitor, but before my hiring at Heads Up, he had found himself a boyfriend. I thought I'd be okay with that, but it became pretty apparent that I was resentful. The Shane I worked side-by-side with was not the Shane I knew from emails and text messages. This guy was smooth, driven, fun, and loved to laugh. I was enraptured by the sound of his voice. He was smart. He was sexy.

My God, was he sexy.

Shane left Heads Up for two reasons that I could tell: His depression and how leadership treated him. As I recall, he had been at the office for longer than two other guys who had received promotions before him. That was a tough pill to swallow for someone with Shane's pride, work ethic, and proven results.

I can't speak much to his depression except on how it impacted me.

He had stopped coming to work, then it was announced that he had resigned. I was hurt. I manifest that hurt through anger. When he came to get some of his things, I didn't want to see him. I felt like he had brought me on board to this place that was terrible, and now he wouldn't even be there to share it with me. (In retrospect, the place wasn't that terrible, but it was nowhere near as great as it could have been.)

We locked eyes and I looked away. While he said his farewells to the others, I got my bag and slipped out. I didn't want to talk to him at all, much less say goodbye.

Rather than hailing a cab to my work site, I took a walk around the block. I suppose on some unconscious level, I wanted him to run after me. I wanted to be pursued like I never had been before. But I looked behind me and he wasn't there.

As I made my way back toward one of the main streets, I saw him. He had a look on his face that suggested he didn't appreciate having to catch up to me.

I don't remember all that was said. That's the tricky part about autobiography. No matter how hard you organize your thoughts, the feelings will always be louder than the script that the Fates wrote for you.

I do remember this: he offered me a ride to my site, and I accepted. I didn't want to, but I did. I knew it would be the last time I'd see him in a while and I didn't want it to end in a huff, too wrapped up in my own feelings to appreciate the moment.

Whatever we talked about in that car felt like old times. It felt like the best of us—our top ten moments of friendship all rolled into one. My icy exterior quickly melted.

But then, in front of my work site, before we departed, he made a comment on my hair. I said I needed a haircut.

He touched me, scratched the back of my head. I melted, then I froze again.

"I don't think this is a good idea," I said.

"Why not?" he asked.

"Do you still have a boyfriend?"

"Yes. I do."

"That's why."

I remember the look on his face was utter disappointment. I don't know what I was supposed to do. I loved this man deeply, but I wasn't going to be his side thing, his "other" man.

How I loved him. How I still do.

The coming weeks and months were no kinder to our friendship. He stayed with his boyfriend. I stayed resentful but tried to climb out of that oubliette.

I invited him to eat at a Thai restaurant on U Street which no longer exists. We made plans. We set them. This was me trying to do the right thing. This was me trying to build a friendship out of something I had hoped would be more but would have to be enough for now. I wanted to tell him I'd gotten over whatever this thing was and was ready to be chill once again.

Those are the things I might have said had he shown up. If our date was for 6pm, then it must have been 6:45pm before I finally gave up and ordered dinner. At the time, I had experienced no greater humiliation than my server's realization that my date wasn't coming.

That food was good, though. I'm still mad they closed that Sala Thai location.

At some point the following week, Shane apologized to me. He told me that his depression kept him in bed the whole day. I was livid. Depression? Kept you in bed? Without a cell phone? You couldn't simply text me and tell me you weren't feeling up to it? Even if you had lied and given a physiological reason, I'd have no choice but to accept it. When it comes to depression, try me. I might get it.

But he didn't tell me until after he stood me up. I carried that with me. I blogged about it.

I blogged about it knowing he would eventually read it, because that's what he does. He checks up on me without checking in with me. He sees what I'm doing without asking how I'm doing.

But I said how angry I was in a very public manner, with no regard to his mental health, pooh-poohing the idea that anyone could be so God-damned *sad* that they couldn't get out of bed. I hate him. I *hate* him.

He believed me, and he emailed me hating me back. I never did read the whole email, but after the first two lines hadn't contained an apology, I figured I needn't read more.

Oh, I could dish it out, but never could I take it. I always had to be the rightest one, even if we were both wrong as two left shoes.

And that was that. Whatever year that was, we never really bounced back. Every now and then, I'd try. In 2008 or so, we reconnected on social media. I thought we were doing good until I realized on a Monday morning that he had been in DC the whole weekend without saying a word. I found out by his posting of the photos.

I guess we weren't really friends and weren't going to be friends. I always—to this day—make sure my friends know when I am going to be in their cities, even if I know we won't be able to link up. I think that's the least I could do as a friend. But a decade ago, that wasn't the space he was in.

By that point, it wasn't about my love for him or my attraction to him. It was really about how I could climb back to where we had been as friends for those months we had also been coworkers.

Years and years later, I created a second Facebook page for professional reasons. On this page, I re-friended a whole bunch of people I had deleted over the years, Shane being among them. I didn't do anything to reconnect, and I don't follow anyone on that page. I'm there to be seen and to convey whatever message I need conveyed professionally.

Then, in late 2015, an episode of *Being Mary Jane* came on that changed my life forever. It's the episode where her friend committed suicide. And for the first time, I really saw myself.

And I wrote this:

More #BeingMaryJane reflections. (December 1, 2015)

(Possible spoilers, please keep scrolling if you haven't seen it.)

Being Mary Jane is a show that I think everyone should watch--but I especially think my white friends should watch it because it gives an interesting, mostly accurate depiction of the black professional class. If you've ever read my books, I definitely view Mary Jane as analogous to Adrian Collins. You really, really want them to succeed, but they keep making terrible life decisions. They are really successful even though you feel they are due for a comeuppance. And they still do believe they are doing the best they can for themselves and their families.

Yesterday's episode broke the fourth wall for me. Rather than comparing the show to my novels, I compared it to my life. For the first time, I felt that I could be Mary Jane. When she mentioned "silent treatment" that was indeed the stick that hit the dog. And I hollered.

I spoke previously about my primordial pain being the absence of important men in my life. I said how when that absence is replicated among the important men currently in my life, it hurts badly.

But what I didn't mention, and what I know to be true of myself, if that the pain inflicted upon me is the pain that I inflict.

I've cut people off. Many people. They are dead to me. I've quit jobs in this manner, too. But in the interpersonal sense, it's easy to decide when you've reach the end of trying, the end of free passes, the end of compromise.

I am not one who apologizes easily because I feel that my patience is long.

I end relationships with people out of a sense of self-care. I reckon that it is indeed self-care in the truest sense that I need to take care of myself before I take care of others. And I do invest a lot into others--to a fault. But it is who I am. The generosity, the care, the gifts, the poems. It's all me.

So is the bitterness, the anger, and the silence.

The silence is me, too.

I realize now, in becoming Mary Jane, that my silence can be deadly. There are times that I mean it. There are times that I didn't mean it but am too ashamed to atone for what I have done, for that would mean an actual, real, adult conversation about the past, who I was, and my primordial pain.

Those roads always lead back to my father. Who he was not, what he did not do, why he did not love me.

Yet, I have become him in many ways in spite of his absence. I don't know the man. My brother says I am more similar to him than I think. So does my mother.

I have to talk more. I have to be honest with my feelings. I have to have the actual, real, adult conversations in the beginning so that the deadly silence won't be my parting gift.

This is most likely why I am alone. Not because I have high standards. Not because I haven't met the right guy. It is because, deep inside, people know. I know that they know. I am a lot to handle and if things don't go just right, the end will be silence.

As Mary Jane said, I have to tell everyone that I will love them no matter how ugly their truth is. But beyond that, I hope that I will be loved in spite of my burdens, in spite of my primordial pain, and in spite of my own ugly, complicated truths.

Shane and I had a conversation after I sent him this message. I apologized to him for how I treated him—a proper apology that only time and wisdom could bring. And he told me about myself. He told me that he's hesitant to get close to me again, because it seems like every time I try, the distance only grows between us. I agreed with him, but that it would take both of us for it to work, because for as many times as I earnestly reached out on social media, there were times he was in my city and never said a word.

He agreed with that assessment as well.

We pledged to do better, but nearly two years have passed and he still hasn't called me back.

I'm at peace with that now. A passion can burn brightly between two people who were never meant to be. The universe never created a pathway between the two of us, be the obstacle an actual person one of us was with, or our own egos or indifference.

I don't know who Shane is—that's for someone else to know, someone who can give him the love that he truly deserves. It was never meant to be me, no matter how electric his touch was on my scalp, no matter how much my heart fluttered when I heard his laugh.

But still, sometimes, against all logic, I hope to see his silhouette in my doorway on those days I am feeling particularly lonely.

For now, social media will have to do. There are no more conversations left between us, as I believe we have finally accepted each other for who we are and what we were.

BILL

JANUARY 31, 2017

On *The Young and the Restless*, the late Katherine Chancellor always called Billy Abbott "Bill." The actress, Jeanne Cooper, made the decision that Katherine would always call the character Bill because he was now a grown man.

I have a coworker who most of my coworkers call by a nickname, Ju-Ju. I call him by his last name, Jones, or Mr. Jones. I find it to be an honor to be called by my last name, and a sign of respect to be called Mister.

He's the last hired, yes. But he's not a runt. He's not a newbie. He is a grown man and I'm not going to call him some nickname. In spite of our collegial environment, it was important for me, as a black man, to acknowledge this other black man. I never called him by this nickname, and I never called him by his first name. Always Jones, or Mr. Jones.

We never talked about this, and I am not his supervisor, so I'm not going to invite myself to a conversation about what I think people should call him. But I do hope he notices that I call him by his name.

BEARING WITNESS

Inasmuch as I can, I want to bear witness to my sexual assault.

I met a man named _______________ years ago. I don't remember how or why we met. It was probably on BlackPlanet.com initially.

He was two years older than me. He was handsome enough, though not a stunner. He was skinny and had a big butt. He was a member of Omega Psi Phi Fraternity, Incorporated, the fraternity I once wanted to be in, then realized I only wanted to be in the members.

He pledged at a chapter not far from here. He had graduated from a DC public school prior to that.

He wore glasses and had a full beard.

We talked a lot about Greek life, as we were both still young in it. I don't remember anything else we spoke about.

I don't even know how I came to know that he liked men. But sure enough, he ended up at my place, making out with me.

It wasn't a rough experience. It wasn't an aggressive experience. But he knew I did not want to have anal sex and he tried to put his penis inside me anyway. I told him I did not want to have anal sex. I told him he could grind on me all he wanted, but he could not put it in. But he tried anyway, without lubricant.

I yelled out in pain and told him to stop. He stopped. He apologized. We continued until we climaxed. But I knew then that he was not the one for me. He left the next morning and I didn't see him again for years, although we kept in touch.

I did not feel like I had been assaulted. I just felt like I lost the lottery and wound up with a creep.

Years passed and I invited him over again. The exact same scenario played out, even though I was even more vocal about not wanting to have anal sex. But he tried anyway, without lubricant. He tried to put his penis inside me, and it hurt.

We stopped. Something inside me changed that evening and I began blaming myself intensely. How could I let this happen twice? How could I let this man violate my body twice? How could I be so stupid?

Years after that, I stopped blaming myself.

The man I was with was a rapist, plain and simple. I had had every right to call the police on him, then or now.

I chose not to because I personally didn't want to go through a potential trial and experience the shame of people telling me what I had already told myself: You knew he was going to try it if you let him? So why did you let him?

Rapists are going to rape. This was never my fault, not even the second time.

No always means no.

I don't know if he's ever done that to anyone since me or before me, but as someone who has experienced this, it's always my own choice to press charges for me, not for anyone else.

I might be heroic at times, but I am not a hero. What worked for me was total separation from him and a vow to speak about rape culture when needed.

That's all I have to say about that.

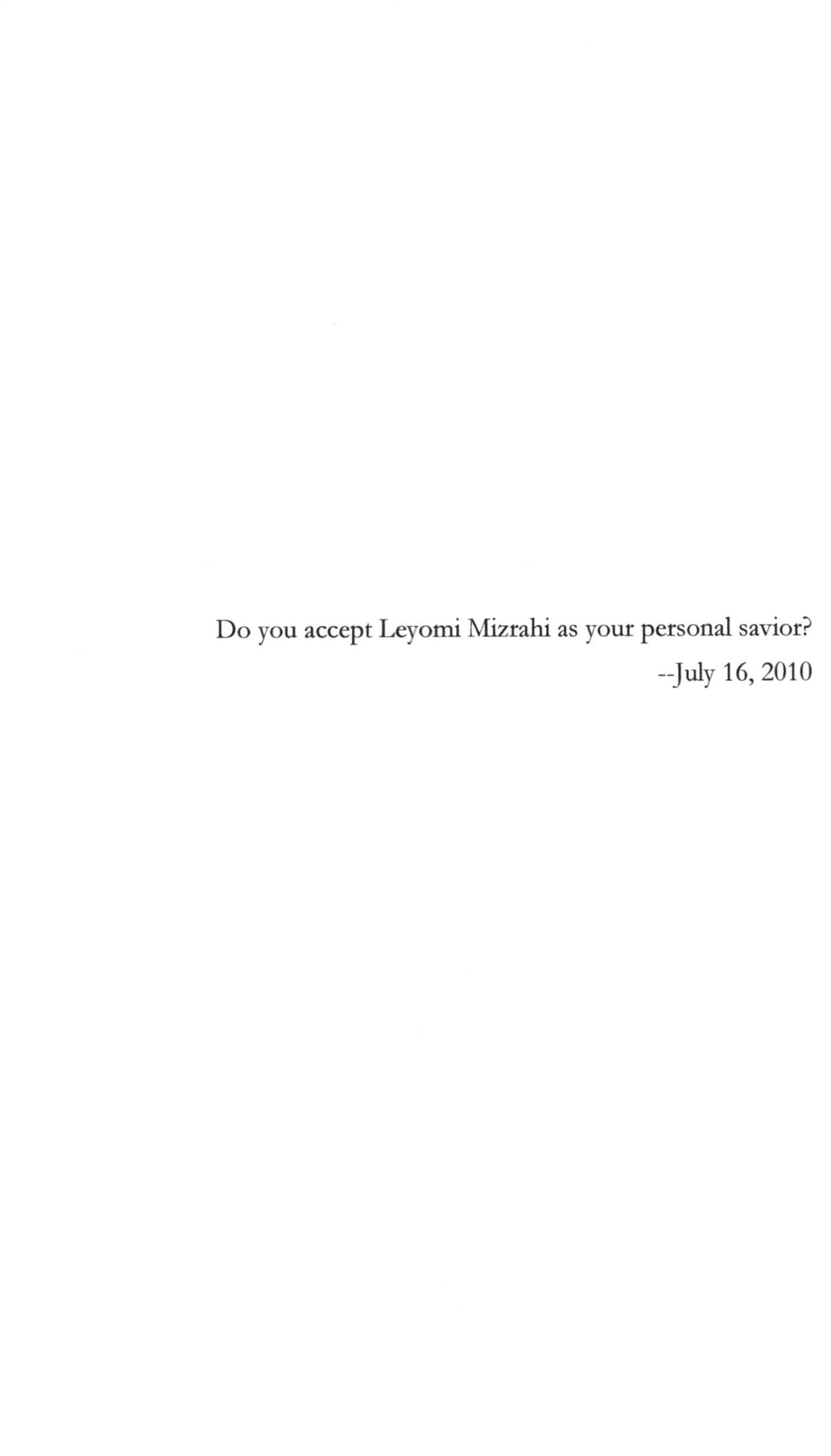

Do you accept Leyomi Mizrahi as your personal savior?

--July 16, 2010

MESSAGE FROM 'THE LEGBA'

2017

Characters: Captain Jason Parks, USAF, and history Professor Brent Haley, both late 30s, African American

Setting: Night. An alley in 2017. A golden space vessel is present.

As the scene opens, the men are bickering.

Brent: You think we're supposed to trust the word of the first alien we see falling out of a golden spaceship? And now she's dead! Jesus! *[Flails arms.]*

Jason: That was no alien. That was a *sister.* She was warning us. And why would aliens name their ship "The Legba?" You think Martians gonna know about West African gods? Brent. This is what we been waiting for. I always knew we'd change the world. I just didn't know it would be like this.

Brent: Jason, come on. *[skeptical]*

Jason: No, you come on. Look what we lived through since high school. 9/11. Stolen elections. School shootings. Dead black bodies in the streets! Donald Trump is the goddamned president!

Brent: We also got marriage equality in every state. Scientific advancements. The internet. And Barack Obama. We lived to see a black man lead this country. And *you* got to call him commander in chief.

Jason: But what if we could live in a world that *we* designed? Believed in *our* gods? Built with *our* architecture? Sang *our* songs? This ship is the key to our freedom.

Brent: Jason, this ship…this is the most powerful weapon on the planet. We can travel anywhere in time. The possibilities are limitless. Why us? Why now?

Jason: Why not us? Why not now? We could stop Trump from being elected. We could save MLK—and Malcolm X! Brent, we could prevent the slave trade. You heard her! "America standing means the end of the world." No slave trade means no America. You know this.

Brent: Listen. If we're successful…we could be wiped away from the timeline completely. No slave trade? No *us*. I didn't wait all this time to be with you only to have it all disappear like it never happened. What we have? It feels mighty real to me. I didn't wait twenty years only to…to lose you. To lose what we could be.

Jason: That's why we gotta do this together! I don't want to lose you, either. Listen: Trayvon Martin. Michael Brown. Philando Castile. This country is after us one by one, two by two, but we can fix this a million by a million. You're the smartest man I know. If this is gonna be my final flight, I don't wanna do it alone. Say you'll do it with me, even if it means…

Brent: Oblivion? *[Pregnant pause between the two; strong stares. Jason looks away.]*

Jason: Yes. Oblivion. Possibly. But what if? [*Pause*] What if this is what we were born to do? Born to *be*?

Brent: You're crazy. But I guess that's why I love you. *[Pauses]* Okay. I'm down. Just to see, at least.

Jason: I love you, too. And I can't do this alone. Now I can fly anything, but I need your knowledge. Tell me where to go. Where in time do we have the best shot at changing the course of history?

Brent: *[Pauses and ponders.]* So many places, so many times. But I think our best shot is 1492. Take out Columbus. Sink the ships. Warn the natives. And send a message to the Spanish crown. Not us. Not here. Not ever.

Jason: My man. *[Embraces, kisses passionately.]* There's nobody else in this world I'd want to dismantle white supremacy with. *[Winks at Brent.]* Now let's go fly this thing. *[Exits to ship.]*

FROM *BEHIND CLOSED DOORS* TO *YOURS IN THE BOND*: TWENTY YEARS OF ADRIAN COLLINS

2018

For months I was determined to include the entirety of my play *Behind Closed Doors* in this book so that I could show my readers the seeds of what would become the Potomac University Series: *Lazarus*, *Covenant*, and *Epiphany*.

However, it's trash.

Like for real. It should not and will not see the light of day.

I will instead tell you the story of *Behind Closed Doors* and the journey of writing the story of Adrian Collins, the boy who was not, and never was, Rashid Darden.

I claim 1998 as the year that I created Adrian Collins, the hero of my novel *Lazarus* and its sequels. I do not know when I really conceived him, but somewhere inside me, for my first two years at Georgetown, was the story of a boy who fell in love with a varsity basketball player and turned his world upside down.

People think I am Adrian Collins, no matter how much I protest to the contrary. Twenty years later, I still insist that I am not Adrian Collins, and that he is purely a work of fiction.

However, all great stories begin with the question "What if?" My play *Behind Closed Doors* is no exception. It is the story of Adrian Collins, a Sophomore at Georgetown, who begins a friendship with a varsity basketball player named Isaiah Aiken. Isaiah is dating a girl named Anne-Marie Sterling, who goes by Marie. They're a campus power couple, perfect in every way.

Isaiah eventually falls in love with Adrian and begins an affair with him. Meanwhile, Adrian is dealing with the aftermath of pledging the Omega Nu Chapter of Beta Chi Phi Fraternity. Although he was officially initiated, he was humiliated during the pledge process when he was outed and forced to drop from an underground line. He also lost his boyfriend, Carlos Ortiz.

None of this happened to me. However, I had three big what-ifs that had everything to do with my undergraduate experience.

First, what if there was a gay Georgetown basketball player? How would that change the very conservative lean of black life on campus? During my first few years at Georgetown, there were no openly gay black men that I knew of, much less any who were scholarship athletes.

Second, what if a gay person pledged a fraternity at Georgetown? My perception of Black Greek Letter Organizations at the time is that they were just as conservative as sports teams. I had not met any openly gay fraternity members at all, much less any who were current collegians. I wanted to interrogate what the aftermath would be to someone who had been outed during their process.

Finally, and most importantly was a very specific question: What if I broke up Isaiah and Marie?

The "real" Isaiah and Marie were a beautiful couple. Marie, in particular, is a great gal and someone I am proud to call a friend twenty years later. She doesn't know that I wanted her man so bad that I wrote a play about it.

Even though the "what if" scenario was based on real people, and Isaiah's face in my head looks like the man he's patterned after, there is nothing else about them which is similar to their relationship or their real lives. Real Isaiah is straight. Real Marie is not a naïve princess.

Carlos Ortiz, too, was visually patterned after a real person on campus, who I also had a huge crush on. I was always too chickenshit to do or say anything about it, by the way. Such is the life of a writer. As the play evolved, so did Carlos. He was renamed Savion Cortez. The name Savion visually looks like Savior, and that was intentional.

Ironically, the real Savion is not a poet, but is in a fraternity—something the fictitious version would never do.

Tasha Bryant in *Behind Closed Doors* evolved into Nina Bradley. I don't recall why I made the change, other than thinking the name Nina was prettier and the surname Bradley was stately.

Hodari Hudgins was an original character who made the transition from *Behind Closed Doors* to the subsequent works. So did Beta members Craig, Aaron, and Jamal—but the homophobic acts I later ascribed to Jamal began with another character named Brian Epps, who was eventually deleted from the narrative.

I was proud of this work when I was finally finished with it during my Junior year. I lived at the Black House when it was located at 1410 36th Street, one block from Georgetown's main gates. I invited a bunch of friends over for a read-through, but only two showed up: the late Maya Buseman-Williams and Amerie Rogers, who later became known to the public as just Amerie, singer of the hits "1 Thing" and "Why Don't We Fall in Love?"

Since there were so few of us, we traded off parts. We read through as much as we could until we gave up. It was a tough slog, although an enjoyable one.

My mentor at the time, novelist Dennis Williams, also read the work. What he told me next changed the trajectory of my career. He said it was okay, but that the real story was the pledge process.

I was skeptical about writing a whole prequel play about Adrian pledging, and I was disappointed that my current work was just "okay."

He told me to consider writing a novel instead, or at least some piece of long fiction to flesh out the backstory until it couldn't be fleshed out anymore.

I put the idea of writing a novel on the backburner and focused on poetry and feature-length essays. I felt I was a pretty good poet in those days—better than I was a playwright—and I decided to ride poetry for as long as I could. My crowning achievement during my senior year was organizing a huge reading called VIP: Verbal Intercession of Poetry. Using BlackPlanet as a tool for recruitment made the difference in the vibe of the event.

Meanwhile, I wrote a piece my senior year called "Representing Ourselves," which was about the black male experience at Georgetown. I conducted surveys, filmed interviews, and wrote extensively on the perceptions of black men from the public as well as how we perceived ourselves and each other. It was pretty good. I felt like maybe someday I could be a real writer, like Dennis.

After graduation, I settled into a mundane 9-to-5 job working for Georgetown at the Office of Alumni and University Relations, now called the Office of Advancement, making about $28,000 a year as an administrative assistant for an Associate Vice President and her minion. I used my newly regimented schedule to devote time to writing the novel. I pretty much stayed in the house for a year—I can't remember going out socially at all for that whole year. I wrote on the weekends and into the evenings, and sometimes in the early mornings.

On Veteran's Day 2002, I finished my first novel and called it *Lazarus.* Strictly speaking, *Lazarus* was intended to be a prequel to *Behind Closed Doors*, which was itself renamed to *Discretion.* However, I had already put my playwrighting days to bed once and for all once *Lazarus* was written. Not only was the experience of writing long fiction exhilarating and empowering, but it was practical. Writing plays would mean a commitment to producing them, and it was a hassle just getting friends to commit to a readthrough. With fiction, I could write it and be done.

My first editor was a coworker and talented writer in her own right, Eman Quotah. I had other coworkers in the print shop who happily printed and bound as many drafts as I asked for.

Dennis introduced me to his agent, who passed on my novel but had good things to say about it. I queried less than ten additional agents over the following months, and each who responded had positive things to say. However, several also said that they didn't feel they had the connections to place a gay novel for publication. Some said that E. Lynn Harris had the market cornered. Others said that bookstores were sadly still homophobic and wouldn't take the risk on a black gay novel.

Because of the generosity of those agents, my decision to self-publish became an easy one. If agents, publishing houses, distributors, and bookstores wouldn't take the risk, then I would. I knew the audience was out there and that they were thirsty for the story of the college boy who pledges the fraternity and tries to keep his orientation a secret from the members.

In 2005, that's exactly what happened. My mother partially invested in my first print run of *Lazarus* and we kept the boxes of books in her basement. I had a book launch at a local jazz club and took orders online. I sold copies at DC Black Pride and Atlanta Black Pride. Although I had shipped a box to a black-owned book distributor, I never saw a cent from them. I later discovered that this company was notorious for ripping off authors in this way. My book was also sold at Lambda Rising Bookstore in the DuPont Circle neighborhood of DC. That store is now closed. Another store, the black-owned Karibu Books, refused to carry my novel, even after Nikki Giovanni's urging. She and I participated in a literary event that the Deltas in DC hosted, and she couldn't understand why Karibu wouldn't carry all of our books. I explained to her that I had submitted my novel to them and had never heard back. The owner sputtered and stammered his way through an explanation, concluding with asking me to resubmit. I did, and they still never carried it. That chain of stores is also now closed.

Although the in-person sales were important and hard-earned, it was my relationship to the Amazon.com platform during this time that made me a life-long supporter. To sell your books on Amazon in those days, you had to register with the site and send them a copy of the book so they could make sure it was real. Then they enrolled you in the program. When an order came in, they would notify you and you'd have to ship a book to their warehouse, where they would then reship it to the customer. The objective was to make that process as efficient as possible so that Amazon would begin requesting boxes of books at a time, rather than single books. Eventually, that happened.

Amazon was good to self-published authors during this time. They remained good to us when they launched CreateSpace, a company which made it much easier to independently publish and distribute. My mentor Dennis, again, came through in a clutch and explained CreateSpace and its print-on-demand technology to me. I rereleased *Lazarus* through CreateSpace and all my subsequent novels were released through them. CreateSpace is now Kindle Direct Publishing.

My friend Frederick Smith, author of several black gay novels himself, is the reason I finally joined the e-book train. While I wasn't personally sure that the market was ripe for e-books, he literally showed me the receipts. I hurriedly placed my novels on Kindle and was stunned when my royalties quadrupled.

After long delays, *Covenant* was released in 2011 and *Epiphany* in 2012. The Potomac University Series was complete, with Adrian and Isaiah riding off in the sunset. Originally, I had a series of spin-off novels planned for him and his friends. Each was to have a David Bowie song as a title.

After *Epiphany* would have been *What in the World*, a novel about how Mohammed Bilal, Adrian's line brother, returns to Algeria and confronts his own issues of racial identity while beginning a long-distance relationship with a woman. Next would have been *The Prettiest Star*, a story about how Nina deals with depression and relationships in her mid-20s while starting a career in DC. *Watch that Man* would have followed soon after, returning the action to Adrian and Isaiah and dealing with Taina's mental illness and eventual death. In this book, too, would have been Jamal seeking custody of Zion.

I scrapped most of those ideas, even though I consider them canonical in the Potomac University Series universe, especially Taina's death, which is mentioned in *Yours in the Bond.*

I parted from those ideas because I didn't want to be known just for dramatic, plot-heavy stories. Yes, stuff happens in my novels and it should be written, but more importantly, people have relationships and they talk. I want my work to be character driven. So any novel that I've planned that became too heavy with plot has ultimately been cancelled or retooled. That includes every book after *Epiphany;* as well as *Blood of a Dark Nation.*

Still, I always knew that I would revisit Adrian Collins. What eventually happened is that I wanted to write a story about two characters who were bizarre, almost grotesque versions of Adrian and Isaiah.

Enter Eustace Dailey and Jeremy Jacob Carter. I knew that they would be Adrian's fraternity brothers and that they would know Isaiah Aiken well. But I asked myself who would these men be while living in Adrian and Isaiah's perfect shadow? If *Lazarus* was about Adrian's inner journey, *Covenant* was about his journey in dyads, and *Epiphany* was about his place in the community, then *Yours in the Bond* would be the next circle away from the community. I hoped for this novel to be about

Adrian's reputation, and what the idea of an Adrian Collins means to the people who know him, as well as people who don't know him well at all.

Yours in the Bond was also my most therapeutic novel. I am not a writer who writes for therapy, but there were remnants of things I was going through that I needed to channel through this novel. While it is still not autobiographical, I can say that Eustace makes decisions that I have also needed to make in my life in order to be a better man.

I believe Eustace is fundamentally asking himself whether or not he is good. Having the model of Adrian Collins in his life can be both positive and overwhelming.

I know how Adrian Collins dies. I know what kind of man he is over the decades of his life. I am not done writing Adrian Collins, but I am close to it. I think there will be one more novel where he is a character, but I won't write it for a while.

Twenty years is a long time to be with a character. I am so grateful that Adrian Collins, his friends, and his fraternity brothers revealed themselves to me two decades ago, and that they chose me to tell their stories. I hope that they live forever and somehow change the world.

AM I A GOOD MAN?

2018

The Doctor: *The answer to my next question. Which must be honest, cold and considered without kindness or restraint. Clara, be my pal. Tell me. Am I a good man?*

Clara: *I… don't know.*

The Doctor: *Neither do I.*

"Into the Dalek." *Doctor Who*. BBC America. August 30, 2014.

Earlier this year, I had a bit of an existential crisis. I had been minding my own business, wandering about the internet and falling down various rabbit holes, from Tumblr to Lipstick Alley to GreekChat and back. On my travels, I discovered that (allegedly) my college classmate (a man) was now dating a male celebrity who was well-known in the black community.

A sense of rage and envy welled up in me, exploded, and turned me upside down. This guy, this *bama* (and he was indeed so back in the day), this saditty prick who now bragged on his Ivy League advanced degrees and designer cars--*he* gets to have a celebrity? He gets to date a pretty dude, a philanthropic dude, a dude who would look better on MY arm?

He hadn't even been out back in the day! He had never stood shoulder to shoulder with me on any matter of the LGBT "community." We'd never had a conversation about identity. He was closeted. He was *ashamed.*

I came out in college for many of the same reasons that I do other things that I do. I wanted to be the person that I needed.

So yes, I came out because there was more room outside of the closet than inside. Yes, I came clean about who I was because I was always proud of who I really was on the inside. And yes, I told the world that I was gay because being someone else was exhausting.

But I also came out because when I stepped foot on Georgetown's campus, there were no other out and visible black gay men there for me to look up to, to learn from, to be my big brother.

I did it knowing that I would be alone, but that I needed to at least be present for the ones who came after.

It was an ethical obligation and a moral imperative. BE OUT, no matter what.

Coming out was easy. Navigating life after it was hard. A dear friend came out to me as bisexual during our senior year--three whole years after I had come out to him--and I resented him for leaving me alone for those three years. I always knew that I had friends, but I didn't feel like I had friends who were going through the same things *with* me, in the proverbial trenches.

A beautiful openly gay black guy came to campus my junior year, and I fell in love with him. He was in love with a sophomore, though. The sophomore had not yet come out to me, and he did his best to strategically shoot his shot, even while I slowly plugged away building the relationship with the freshman. That sophomore later became my nemesis, even though we would later have somewhat of a reconciliation as adults. The revelation was a scandal, though, and it sent me reeling for a while.

I later fell for another guy, the first of many, many, *many* other guys who I thought I was quietly building something with, only to have him gaslight me and pretend that there was no *there* there.

Dude. *There* was there. He knew it and the world saw it, from our rosy-cheeked, bashful glances toward one another to the late-night strolls and conversations about everything and nothing at all.

Georgetown men were notorious closet cases. But then there was me. I was always different. I was always special. I was always just a little bit more outer than you, soooo....

Perhaps nobody likes the smug social justice warrior who speaks in the tongues of those he has read rather than walking in the shoes of those around him. Because, and forgive my crassness, at least those around him were getting their nut. And so it would seem, they weren't just getting their nut with just anybody, now they were getting their nut in the broadcast television niggerati.

Where was my piece of the pie? Why not me? Five books later, why am I still so alone and feeling unwanted? Where was my man? I worked *hard* for this.

The realization hit me harder than I imagined the pavement would have had I leapt from Copley Hall that day: I am not a good man.

A good man would not covet the things, people, or life of someone else. I don't even think of this classmate unless someone else brings him up, so why am I in such a rage? I didn't want the things that he flaunts, until this very moment.

In 2005, black gay culture hit somewhat of a zenith--not as big as the *Moonlight* zenith, but we reached a point of saturation of good, quality gay black content, from Prides and circuit parties to gay black television and film. And I was in the middle of it all, with my writer comrades, just pumping the culture full of good work.

I didn't think of my classmate then. I didn't covet what he had then, even though he already had way more than me.

In 2005, I never felt freer. I was alive. I was surrounded by people who loved me and supported my career.

But somewhere along the way, that reality splintered like an iPhone screen. The writers didn't write as much. The bloggers diversified and then dissipated. *Noah's Arc* was canceled. It seemed like the empire we were building as a community just withered away.

It came back in a major way, of course, but very few of those stalwart builders of just 13 years ago are still around, and fewer still have the prominence those years would suggest.

What was my classmate doing in those same 13 years to deserve the level of access he now had?

Therein was my problem: I felt owed. Not just a boyfriend. I felt entitled to status and access, because I had dared to be myself. I felt as though my coming out was a gift to others that hadn't been repaid to me in the form of a perfect life. I felt like if I came out, that alone made me a good person because I was the one who had to suffer through the things I'd experienced.

I've received hate mail, anonymous and otherwise, from neighborhood busybodies and fraternity brothers. I've had a mentor out me to a friend and housemate, only to apologize, then turn his back on me many more times over. I've felt real fear, from the streets to my classroom. Yet, I'm still here. Struggling to survive, yet here.

I was envious of a man I never liked over a man I'd never have and a life I didn't really want at all.

That made me trash, and I knew it.

I became introspective and really began to contemplate what it meant to be good. Episodes of *Doctor Who* have that sort of impact on your life if you allow them to.

I began to question my motives for everything. Why was I a teacher? Why did I go to Georgetown? Why did I date who I dated? Why wouldn't I date who I haven't?

I've always been a philosopher, so those questions only took me back to answers that I knew. Yet, I still didn't feel like I was a good man.

I no longer felt envious of this classmate. I felt badly that I had envied him. He was literally just living his life and happened to date someone that was attracted to him. It makes no difference to me.

And that was the best epiphany I would have through those months of doing the work: It makes no difference.

The word difference has many definitions, and when we deconstruct them all, each definition applied in this case:

- a point or way in which people or things are not the same: *me and my classmate are not the same. that doesn't make us unequal*

- a disagreement, quarrel, or dispute: *my classmate and I have no quarrel. his choices have no bearing on my life*

- a quantity by which amounts differ: a*s human beings living on this earth, there is no quantity by which we differ. his money, his lover, his access make him no more a human being than i am*

And somewhere in that reflection, I found peace.

I dated someone this year who was beautiful and loving and made me feel attractive. Yet, it was not enough. I resolved to not block the blessing of whoever in this universe was out there who deserved him, and we very cordially parted romantic ways. I appreciated very much that he loved me in the body I have and the bank account that I own. He didn't need me to drive a designer car or have a Hollywood job. I had the man I was supposed to, for the time period I was supposed to, even though it was brief.

I also have come very close to publishing not one, but two new books. In that peace, I rediscovered who I was and what my next steps would be. I am a novelist who is figuring out how to be a full-time novelist who doesn't covet what others possess, no matter what I did in my life to feel like I deserved them.

Coming out doesn't entitle me to anything but the freedom to be out. Nothing more, nothing less. There is no prize for being the person that I needed.

Last night, I went to a neighborhood bar and met up with a bunch of old work buddies, including the one I called Work Bae: the straight man whose bathwater I'd drink if I could. I can't say that I was ever in love with him--not a sincere, passionate love, at least. More like a crush that I was happily resigned to be swept away in. He, in turn, was more than happy to have that sort of admiration.

In an interesting twist, I'd brought New Work Bae, also known as White Work Bae, with me to the bar. Hey, a guy's got to have a crush target for the eight hours he's at work, right?

The joking between Work Bae and I commence and he's teasing me about this new guy. And I tell him "Look, you got married and I had to move on. You need to let me go now; I have a good thing over here."

And he says "Man you were my cinnamon apple! How could you do this to me? It's like that?!" He calls me his cinnamon apple at least a dozen times at the top of his lungs in this bar.

I was legitimately mortified. I don't embarrass easily, but I know my face had to have been redder than a Kappa blazer. Tears were literally streaming from my eyes I was so embarrassed. Yet, I was endeared.

We drank more and laughed more and posed for pictures. I asked our friend to give us a countdown, and on three, I turned my head like I would kiss him on the cheek. He recoiled and laughed and said I already kissed him once. Our friend said, "And you never washed your cheek again, did you!?"

Fact check: It was actually him that kissed me, but who's counting?

Later in the evening, he pulled me to the side, hugged me (a few times), looked me in my eyes, and said: "Darden, I really miss you. You're my guy. You always looked out for me and helped me and made me a better person. I could rely on you when I needed it. You're one of the best people I know. You're a great man."

I smiled, nodded, and said "Thank you."

Before that moment, I hadn't thought much for the past few months on whether or not I was a good man. It shaped up to be less of an existential crisis than I thought I would be. I was content to just be a man who attempts to keep getting better every day and maybe let God sort out the rest when it's time.

But maybe God wanted me to know more, sooner.

Clara: *You asked me if you were a good man and the answer is I don't know. But I think you try to be and I think that's probably the point.*

ABOUT THE AUTHOR

Rashid Darden is an award-winning novelist local to Washington, DC, and Northampton County, NC. His best work is his next work.

Please visit him at www.OldGoldSoul.com or any social media at the handle @RashidDarden.

Portrait by Reginald Cunningham. @KidNoble

LAZARUS

RASHID DARDEN

Also by

RASHID DARDEN

The big man on campus has a secret…

ADRIAN is handsome, brilliant, and devoted to serving others. Under the cool exterior, however, he is tormented and unfulfilled. Abandoned by his father and emotionally distant from his mother, he feels alone – adrift on campus - until he meets SAVION. With rhymes dripping from his lips like honey, Savion has just what Adrian needs: stability, maturity, and love. Although their friendship is filled with peaks and valleys, their relationship is threatened by Adrian's biggest challenge: BETA CHI PHI.

Finding the appeal of pledging his father's fraternity irresistible, Adrian decides to take the plunge and pledge Beta Chi Phi in an attempt to fill the void in his heart, even after his relationship with Savion blossoms. Almost immediately, Adrian is thrust headlong into a world of mind games, controlled behavior, and strokes from the paddle--tempered with the brotherhood that bonds men in times of adversity. Adrian knows that he must keep his relationship with Savion a secret at all costs, for if his new-found family were to learn the truth, he may have to choose…

The one he loves…or his brothers.

LAZARUS

Volume I

of the Potomac University Series

COVENANT
RASHID
DARDEN

Also by

RASHID DARDEN

Who will be the first to break?

ADRIAN is on a mission to heal himself from his emotional wounds. Though he is fresh off the "burning sands" of Beta Chi Phi, he suddenly finds himself alone. He sets himself to the task of reconciling with his parents while forging his own path as a newly "out" man on campus – no easy feat when some fraternity brothers still harbor animosity toward him.

ISAIAH is struggling to redefine himself. He is a student, basketball player, and boyfriend to a beautiful young lady. But who does he want to be? Isaiah's friendship with Adrian awakens new feelings within him – feelings that are both exciting and terrifying.

Over the course of one summer these two men are united as friends - and more. What happens between them is kept secret, even from their closest friends. As they cross each other's paths on the close-knit campus, they both long to finish what they started during that long, humid summer. Still, they made a promise...

COVENANT

Volume II
of the Potomac University Series

EPIPHANY

RASHID DARDEN

Also by

RASHID DARDEN

ISAIAH is head over heels in love with his boyfriend and isn't afraid to let the world know it. His unwavering love threatens his future as a professional basketball player. Though he is being forced to choose between the love of his life and his career, it appears that he could be making a decision which could irrevocably affect his future.

Meanwhile, ADRIAN has unfinished fraternity business. As a Big Brother for the first time, he has an obligation to uphold the chapter's sacred traditions, yet feels a responsibility to end the cycle of violence.

Friendships will dissolve. Rivals will return. Secrets buried in LAZARUS and maintained in COVENANT will finally explode.

EPIPHANY

Volume III

of the Potomac University Series

The Life and Death of Savion Cortez

Poems by

Rashid Darden

Also by

RASHID DARDEN

THE LIFE AND DEATH OF SAVION CORTEZ is the debut volume of poetry presented by Rashid Darden on the topics of love and loss. It is a companion to the Potomac University Series that interrogates the trilogy through the eyes of one of its most polarizing characters.

THE LIFE AND DEATH OF SAVION CORTEZ

The Poetic Companion to the Potomac University Series

Available now
www.oldgoldsoul.com

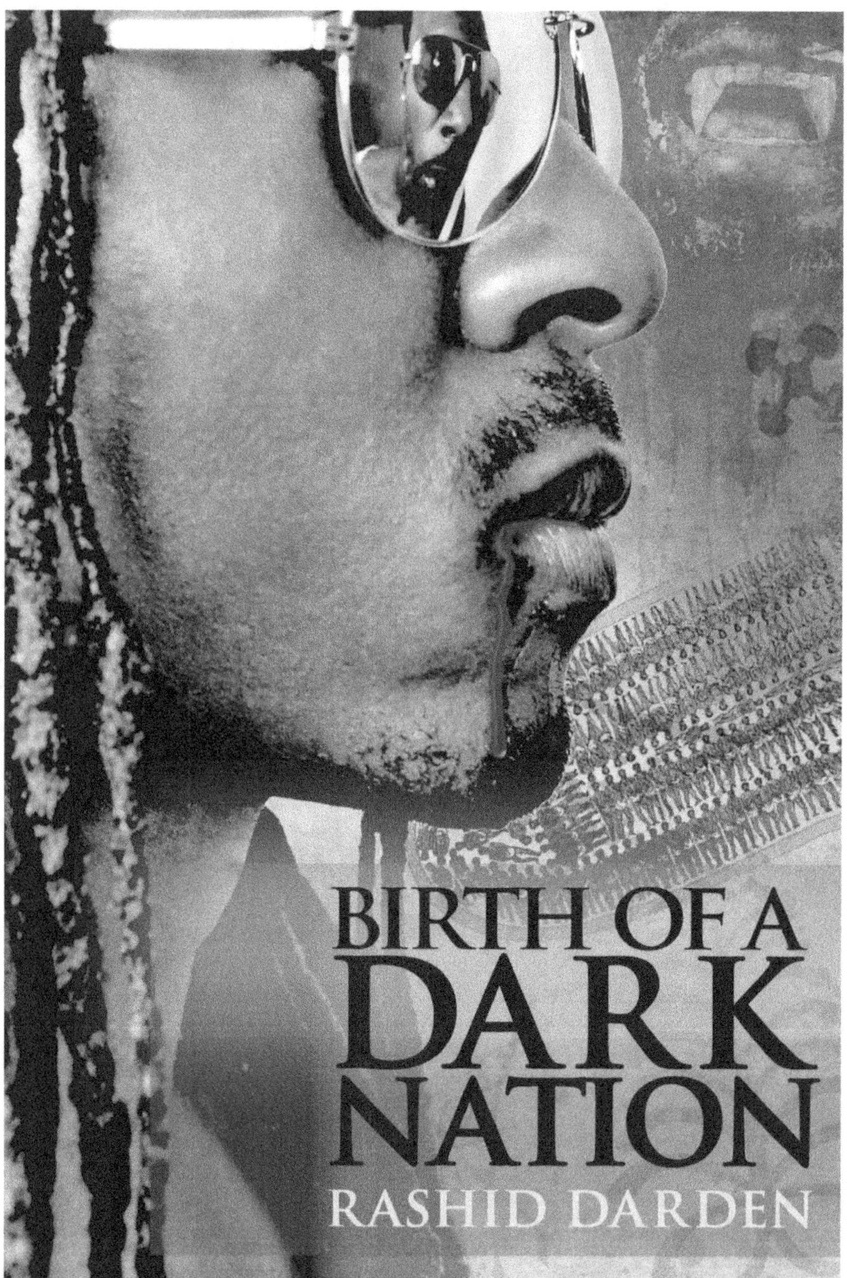
BIRTH OF A
DARK
NATION
RASHID DARDEN

Also by

RASHID DARDEN

JUSTIN KENA never knew his own strength. He was an average guy stuck working at a mediocre nonprofit in Washington, DC, unsure exactly where his next professional steps would take him. He was awkward, bored, lonely, and bordering on depression. With nothing to lose, he accepts a proposition from his friendly neighborhood corner boy that forever transforms his life.

A guru and a hustler all at once, DANTE earns Justin's trust and ushers him into a new and terrifying world just under the surface of the one he's always known. In this world, men and women are nothing more than food for day-walking vampires and housing for sinister demons. This lifestyle consumes Justin until he's not even sure he could turn back–or if he even wants to.

Over the span of centuries and thousands of miles, from slave coffles in West Africa to the antebellum South; from the black sand beaches of Dominica to the back alleys of the nation's capital, Justin and Dante will live by the precepts of justice and redemption while satisfying their most carnal urges:

A lust for blood…and a thirst for life.

BIRTH OF A DARK NATION

The thrilling first installment of the Dark Nation Series

Available now
www.oldgoldsoul.com

YOURS IN THE BOND

RASHID DARDEN

Also by

RASHID DARDEN

EUSTACE DAILEY has a Harvard degree, an artist's eye, an active social life, and more money than he knows what to do with at his age. He should feel on top of the world, but instead, he constantly second-guesses his choices–especially when it comes to JJ.

JEREMY JACOB CARTER has confidence, charisma, the perfect girlfriend, and only a year left in law school. He is supposed to have it all, but a chance connection with Eustace threatens to undermine everything he worked so hard for.

Along with their fraternity brothers MILES JOHNSON, IAN KENNEY, and ADRIAN COLLINS (from the Potomac University Series), the men stumble through their adult years in search of brotherhood, friendship, love, and purpose.

YOURS IN THE BOND

An exciting, new spin-off from the Potomac University Series!